Does Christianity

Really Work?

Dr. Edgar offers to all a Christianity of logic, truth and transcendence—an ultimate balm that will both heal and protect against the harsh realities of life. He does not hesitate to confront the difficult questions that challenge our faith in times of doubt while also giving his readers a vision of a society transformed by Christian leadership.

Al Sikes
Former Chairman, FCC and author of *Culture Leads Leaders Follow*

From now on, when skeptics ask, 'Where in the world has Christianity done any good,' we have a powerful and convincing reply in my friend, William Edgar's newest book. Bill debunks myths and blows the dust off of little known historical facts about the impact of the Gospel in a hurting world, giving the reader a solid grasp on the positive influence of Christian principles during the darkest of times. Best of all, *Does Christianity Really Work?* is a guide to us as we promote peace, joy, and justice in our broken world. For our times and all times, I highly recommend this remarkable book.

Joni Eareckson Tada
Joni and Friends International Disability Center

William Edgar addresses one of the main questions that sceptics and seekers have about Christianity—does it actually work? Looking at some issues from a positive perspective (the good that Christianity has done, and continues to do) and others from a negative (the alleged harm it is supposed to have brought), Edgar gives reasoned, evidenced and clear answers. This is a good primer for the seeker or the sceptic.

David Robertson
Pastor, St Peter's Free Church of Scotland, Dundee & trustee of SOLAS, Centre for Public Christianity

The Big Ten:
Critical Questions Answered

Does Christianity

Really Work?

WILLIAM EDGAR

SERIES EDITORS
JAMES N. ANDERSON AND GREG WELTY

William Edgar is Professor of Apologetics at Westminister Theological Seminary in Philadelphia, and an accomplished jazz pianist. He is married to Barbara and they have two children, William and Deborah.

paperback ISBN 978-1-78191-775-6
epub ISBN 978-1-78191-893-7
Mobi ISBN 978-1-78191-894-4

Mobi
Published in 2016
by
Christian Focus Publications Ltd,
Geanies House, Fearn, Ross-shire
IV20 1TW, Scotland
www.christianfocus.com

Cover design by Paul Lewis

Printed by Bell and Bain, Glasgow

MIX
Paper from responsible sources
FSC www.fsc.org FSC® C007785

CONTENTS

Dedication

For Luder and Mary Lou Whitlock
Eminently practical Christians
The very best friends

Preface

oes the Christian faith work? Is it practical?
For a good many advocates today the fact that
it works is the very essence of the gospel. If you
peruse the religion section in a bookstore or at the airport,
you will find claims such as 'Jesus can make you a better
you', or that you can end your depression by applying
a few simple gospel principles. In many countries around
the world the message of the 'health and wealth gospel' is
proclaimed. For some, the impact the Christian faith has
had in history is one of the primary proofs of its veracity.
And indeed, there is an impressive record of social and
cultural improvement based on the Christian message.
One readily thinks of health care, women's rights, glorious
art and music, governments with checks and balances, the
abolition of slavery, and so much more.

However, two questions immediately come to mind that give us pause. First, what about the dramatic failures attributable to Christians? Corruption has dogged the clergy from ancient times till today. Apartheid was justified by some Reformed Christians based on the doctrine of providence. So was chattel slavery. It took much too long for believers to find slavery and human trafficking contrary to Scripture. On the whole, the church was slow, very slow to respond to the cruel messianic ambitions of the Third Reich. Both the Hutus and the Tutsis claimed to be practicing Christians, yet the death toll in the genocide is in the hundreds of thousands. Facing these issues, it would be too facile to say, 'But they were the wrong kinds of Christians.' Certainly these great evils came because of a failure to live up to the will of Christ as found in the pages of the New Testament. But the truth is, Christians have at times been on the wrong side of the moral ledger.

The second question is a deeper one. Does the truth of the Christian message depend on its achievements? Is the measurable triumph of the gospel a requirement for its veracity? This is a harder question than may first appear. Should we, in effect, subject God to our human criteria, things such as visible signs, evidence, data, and so forth? Is He not self-defining, self-attesting? It would have seemed an insulting affront had Moses, upon hearing

'I am that I am', asked for more evidence than God's Word itself. And yet, the gospel does not call for *fideism*, the notion that belief needs no justification. Appeals in the Bible are never to the 'leap of faith', without any basis. Even Moses stood before a burning bush. Furthermore, the Lord Jesus told us He would build His church on the rock of apostolic faith (Matthew 16:18).[1] His church is surely not merely invisible. There must be evidence for its effectiveness.

This little book is an attempt to recognize some of the achievements throughout history attributable to the Christian faith, without at the same time isolating those achievements from the person and character of the God who is ultimately behind them. And it also wants to recognize that where there have been failures, some of them dreadful, the fault is not with the gospel but with sinful believers. Sin is a far more serious plague than most people today are ready to acknowledge. But this plague may be healed. Sin can be forgiven. That, in fact, is the true heart of the Christian message. Christ came 'once for all at the end of the ages to put away sin by the

---

1. Bible references such as 'Matthew 16:18' refer to the Bible book called 'Matthew', to the sixteenth chapter of that Bible book, and specifically to the eighteenth verse of that chapter. Thus, 'bookname xx:yy' refers to chapter xx, verse yy of bookname. Most versions of the Bible have a table of contents with page numbers to help you locate each book by name.

sacrifice of himself' (Hebrews 9:26). While that work of redemption is accomplished, it is still being applied.

Acknowledgments

A number of people have contributed to making this a far better text than it might have been. I would like to thank Willie MacKenzie, Director of Publishing at Christian Focus Publications, for first suggesting this book. He has had a hand in a number of my writings, and I am grateful for his friendship. I would also like to thank James Anderson and Greg Welty for their thorough, learned, and meticulous editing. All of their suggestions have been welcomed. If there remain deficiencies, they are my own and not theirs. I also would like to thank Westminster Theological Seminary for giving me a schedule that allows for significant writing time. It continues to be a joy and a privilege to work here. Finally, as ever, and always true, I want to thank my wife Barbara for her faithful, loving and appropriately critical support throughout this project. Thanks, my love!

Introduction

Os Guinness once said: 'Christianity is not true because it works; it works because it is true.'[1] You might ask, what difference does it make whether a religion or a philosophy works, as long as it is true? But in the case of Christianity it matters enormously whether it works, since it claims not only to be the truth but to produce measurable, positive effects. Jesus said He was going to build His church on the solid foundation of the apostolic confession, and that the gates of hell would not prevail against her (Matthew 16:18). I take this to mean at the very least that the church, where the Christian faith is kept, will progress throughout history. Where the church is strong, not only spiritual

---

1. Os Guinness, *God in the Dark: The Assurance of Faith Beyond the Shadow of a Doubt* (Wheaton: Crossway, 1996), p. 77.

benefits should follow but social improvements as well. And nothing will be able to defeat her. Furthermore, the gospel is the good news that Jesus Christ has come to save His people, and the apostle Paul describes this gospel as the power of God for salvation to everyone who believes (Romans 1:16). Taking the term 'salvation' in the broadest sense, which is Paul's intention, we should expect to see all kinds of amelioration at least where people profess faith (1 Thess. 1:5). And as the gospel spreads, down through the ages, there ought to be assessable advancement (Acts 1:8). How can we affirm that it works, without saying it is basically a pragmatic religion or simply a moral system?

Is the Christian faith practical? Does it do any good? Objections to any such claims are common. Sometimes they are put in the starkest terms. The late Christopher Hitchens titled one of his most explosive books, *God Is Not Great: How Religion Poisons Everything*. In it he attacks (mostly) the so-called Abrahamic religions from just about every conceivable angle.[2] Just to pick one or two examples, he claims that Catholicism, along with Islam, has slowed down any progress against the HIV/AIDS disease because of objections to birth-control. Indeed he says the two religions have proclaimed the pandemic as

---

2. Christopher Hitchens, *God Is Not Great: How Religion Poisons Everything* (New York: Hachette/Twelve Books, 2009).

a judgment of God against homosexuals, which cannot yield any progress toward its cure. Hitchens also touts atheists and unbelievers as being at least as effective against human suffering as believers. He cites the case of slavery in North America, where people such as Abraham Lincoln (whom he describes as an agnostic) were more effective than the abolitionists in the fight for its eradication. Authors like Hitchens have produced a veritable cottage industry of materials attacking the claims of religion. Some of it is entertaining, some undoubtedly true, and much of it highly questionable. But it is worth sorting out some of the more pertinent critiques set forth before dismissing their screeds altogether.

To be sure, during various periods of history the church has been the problem, not the solution for human distress. One oft-cited example includes the medieval wars known as the Crusades, which critics call acts of terror in the name of religion. While these holy wars are complex and caused by many different motives, some aspects of them are surely justly indicted. Despite some of the glories of medieval culture, certain abuses were indeed practiced, for which believers today are rightly ashamed. Many would point the finger at the agency of the church known as the Inquisition, which, at its worst, promoted violent repression of perceived heresy.

Voltaire (1694–1778) singles out the Inquisition as both cruel and ridiculous. In his philosophical novel, *Candide*, he has the Inquisitor arrest Candide and his philosopher friend Pangloss for refusing to believe in original sin. Dostoyevsky, a century later, tells a parable on 'The Grand Inquisitor' in which the Cardinal of Seville imprisons Jesus Christ for preaching freedom to the people.

Again, the real story of the Crusades and the Inquisition is somewhat more involved than these critics would allow, though surely some of the abuses were real. One could multiply such examples. Did not the church comfort colonialist efforts? Did not many Christians harbor chattel slavery and even defend it theologically? Did parts of the church not close their eyes to the Nazi persecutions in the twentieth century? And what about Apartheid in South Africa which was justified by Dutch Reformed churchgoers? Also, according to some historians the church has consistently slowed down the progress of science, impeding the advancement of human understanding of the world around us.

On a more psychological level, many have plausibly noted that religion can be manipulative. Targets for critique would have to include the television evangelists who end their programs with tawdry appeals for funding: 'Give until it hurts', as one refrain has it. One can also think of missions to poor people, handicapped children, and so forth, where a picture of a tearful child is accompanied by appeals, saying your modest contribution can educate or heal such a youngster for life. A few of them have practiced embezzlements of donated funds. A number of the so-called healing ministries have been exposed as shams, with the testimonies uncovered as false, and the preachers revealed to be fraudulent.

CASE CLOSED?

How fair are these observations? How representative are they of the core of Christian religious belief and their results in practicality? It is tempting to answer in three ways. First, to refute the evidence. Upon close examination, a good many of the claims of the critics of religion can be shown to be dubious. Eastern Orthodox theologian David Bentley Hart said of *God Is Not Great*: 'On matters of simple historical and textual fact … Hitchens's book is so extraordinarily crowded with errors that one soon gives up counting them.'[3] The same is often true of other one-sided assessments of the connection of religion to social evils. It is critically important to get the facts right.

Yet, we should not move too fast here. If Christopher Hitchens was driven by his one-sided agenda, there are

---

3.   In *First Things*, May 2010 [http://www.firstthings.com/article/2010/04/believe-it-or-not].

others who have no particular axe to grind, yet who really do uncover some actual abuses by the church. For example, as the evidence piles up, we unfortunately find numerous cases of the indifference, if not the complicity, of the church with the Nazi occupation of Europe, including the persecution of Jews, Gypsies, homosexuals, handicapped persons, etc. This too is very complex, almost never black and white. But it happened. Take the case of Cardinal Gerlier of Lyon. He found himself conflicted between his dread of Nazi paganism and his desire to protect France from violence. So he chose cooperation with the Vichy government, the puppet of the Nazis. He believed that the most helpful, indeed the most Christian approach for France during the war was loyalty to Marshal Pétain, the head of that government, and a Nazi collaborator. Gerlier was as anti-racist and anti-pagan as a Catholic ought to be, yet was unable fully to see the evils perpetrated by the Third Reich, at least until the very end. While understandable, the collaborationist approach was reprehensible.[4] Apologies and amends are called for, not cover-ups.

A second and very important item to add here is that the Bible portrays our world as dreadfully corrupt. On almost every page we see a world that was once beautiful

---

4. See Sylvie Bernay, *L'Église de France face à la persécution des juifs 1940-1944* (Paris: CNRS Éditions, 2012).

and peaceful at the creation, now fallen and in misery. Murders, abuse, lying, corruption; these are daily fare. The Bible tells us evil is not primarily 'out there' but 'in here'. Jeremiah 17:9 describes the heart as 'desperately wicked' (KJV). Previous to the great flood, the book of Genesis describes human wickedness as 'great in the earth, and that every intention of the thoughts of his [man's] heart was only evil continually' (Genesis 6:5). 'All is vanity', the Preacher tells us in Ecclesiastes (1:2,14; 2:1; etc.). This is in no way to defend, let alone justify sinful behavior. Nor should it let the church off the hook. It's just plain realistic. To believe otherwise is to live in a fool's paradise.

The Bible not only predicts the success of the church, but also the darkening presence of evil in the world. In the parable of the net, Jesus likens the kingdom of heaven to a great fish net cast into the sea catching fish of all kinds. Just as the fishermen sort out the good fish from the bad, so, at the end of the age, He tells us, angels will come to separate evil ones from the righteous (Matthew 13:47-50). Over and over, the Bible predicts the coming of great evil into the world. The days between the first century and the end will be filled with wars, persecutions, false messiahs and hatred (Matthew 24:6ff.). The apocalyptic Book of the Revelation announces catastrophes, tribulations and judgments until the end. If Christianity really works, it will have to be right about the evil of the world. What we are looking for, then, cannot be the total eradication of evil from the face of the earth. Both the good and the bad will coexist until the end. Jesus referred to the wheat and the weeds growing up together, making it difficult to sort things out until the day of judgment (Matthew 13:24-30).

WHAT ARE WE LOOKING FOR?

Does that mean we can always hide behind the reality of evil, throw up our hands and be satisfied with little or nothing? No! So, then, how do we answer the question, does Christianity really work? The third approach is to find many ways in which the Christian faith has been positive, despite the reality of evil. Here, then, is how we shall proceed. We will take various examples of stumbling blocks to faith. In each case we will stress the basic Christian principles involved in the diagnosis and the cure. As we will see, however real, however besetting the problem may be, the fundamental problem is that men and women are not right with God. The Bible describes this separation with God in a variety of ways. One of them is *sin*. This word, not very well understood today, refers to the guilt of the human race for having refused to follow God and His ways, thinking it better to follow its own way. This liability has separated us from God our creator. The immediate consequence of sin is to render us enemies with God (or, rather, to render Him enemies with us), with the ultimate result, death. The greatest need of all, then, is to be reconciled to God by the forgiveness of sins. Yes, social betterment matters a great deal. But being right with God matters even more. Social betterment follows rather than precedes being right with God.

There is a story in the New Testament that illustrates this sequence well. When Jesus was beginning His public ministry, people came from all over to hear Him and to watch Him perform healings. One incident occurred which tells us about this priority. As recorded in three of the four gospels, Jesus is teaching in a home to a very large crowd.[5] Suddenly a group of four men with a friend on a stretcher, paralyzed, opened up the roof and lowered their friend down directly into Jesus' presence. He turned to the man and said: 'Son, your sins are forgiven.' To the disgruntled religious leaders this was blasphemy: only God can forgive sins. But to prove to them that He was God He asked which was harder, to forgive sins or to heal the man from his paralysis. Both are impossible, of course, except to God. So He then

---

5.   Matthew 9:1-8; Mark 2:1-12; Luke 5:17-26.

told the man to get up and walk home. While Christ is equally committed to forgiving our sins and to healing our infirmities, there is a priority nevertheless to getting right with God.

Only when we have a good grasp of what we should be looking for can we go and find out whether it is there or not. What we find is that the world is in a great mess because of human folly. And we find that our fundamental need is freedom from liability. We also find the promise that God cares deeply about all of our needs, including our need for health, food, clothing, good relationships, work, and so forth. But we learn of His priorities and of the order of things in His work. First, he wanted to secure a way for us to be right with Him, and free of guilt. He accomplished this through the death and resurrection of His Son, Jesus Christ, who took our place, being punished so that we would not have to be. Next, He will ensure that, in His own timing, we will also be given whatever else we need, including life after death. There is the biblical order. To look for another is to depart from the claims of the Christian religion.

Jesus Christ, the centerpiece of the Christian religion, in one sense has accomplished all that is needed for us, and in another sense is still actively applying His power to the remaining agenda. This principle is sometimes known as the 'already-not-yet' of the gospel.

What this means is that while all of the power was fully secured by the death and resurrection of Christ, the full implementation of this power, particularly in areas such as social betterment, is deployed gradually in human history. Finally, we will look for the places where that power really does work itself out in history in ways that ought to be identifiable. Thus, we will argue that despite the numerous setbacks and weaknesses of the church, nevertheless we can point to substantial progress.

In what follows we shall ask a number of questions which appear to raise doubts about the veracity of the Christian message because it does not seem to be working. These questions are rather different from one another. And they are hardly exhaustive. But they do reflect the qualms held by many—qualms which deserve some answers.

1

Peace-Making: A Time to Resist

A RELIGION OF PEACE?

The garden behind the United Nations in New York features several statues and sculptures—gifts from different countries. One of the best known, a gift from the Soviet Union in 1959, features a man holding a hammer in one hand and a sword in the other, which he is making into a plow. The title, 'Let Us Beat Swords into Plowshares', is taken from Isaiah 2:4. There is a certain irony here, in that the Soviet Union at that point was the bitter enemy of the American-led countries in the Cold War. Officially the Soviets were atheists, while America was at least culturally Christian.

Nearly all of mankind longs for peace. But how to obtain it? Surely, if the Christian faith is true, then there ought to be evidence that it is a religion that promotes peace. Certainly, bringing peace is what the Bible claims. Jesus praised the artisans of peace in His list of the beatitudes: 'Blessed are the peacemakers, for they shall be called sons of God' (Matthew 5:9). The terms translated 'peace' are used nearly 370 times throughout the Bible. 'To set the mind on the flesh is death', Paul tells us, 'but to set the mind on the Spirit is life and peace' (Romans 8:6). 'Strive for peace with everyone', we are enjoined (Hebrews 12:14). The Lord is often called 'the God of peace', a nomenclature made throughout the Scriptures (see Romans 15:33; 2 Corinthians 13:11; Hebrews 13:20).

Before we look at evidence for Christian peace-making in the world, a reminder is in order. Jesus is the ultimate peacemaker. He came first to establish peace where it was most needed, between people and God. As we mentioned earlier, the gospel is above all a message of peace with God, through His Son, Jesus Christ (Acts 10:36). If our deepest need is to be reconciled with our Maker, then the gospel gives us ultimate peace (Romans 5:1).

This kind of peace is not first and foremost a feeling. Rather, it is a reality, the reality of freedom of access to God. God, our enemy, has made Himself our friend. Through His pain and suffering on the cross, Jesus Christ opened the way to God the Father. Why did He have to pay such a price? Because our enmity is culpable, and there is only one way our guilt can be erased: the punishment required by justice. When Jesus hung on the cross and exclaimed: 'My God, my God, why have you forsaken me?' He was feeling the full anger of God against the sin of humanity. The only just consequence of our guilt is death. And, marvelously, Jesus was willing to die for us, to become sin for us, so that we could become new creatures in Christ (2 Corinthians 5:17, 21). Then He was raised up to life, 'for our justification' that is, for our acquittal (Romans 4:25).

Here is the 'already' of the already-not-yet. Jesus can say to His followers: 'I have said these things to you that in me you may have peace. In the world you will have tribulation. But take heart; I have overcome the world' (John 16:33). Quite a statement! Does this mean that any time someone comes to Christ he or she will know nothing but peace and quiet? Of course not. Christ's overcoming the world was accomplished once-and-for-all on the cross, yet the full effects of that victory will not be felt until the very end. He Himself predicted tribulation in history until the close of the age, as we have seen.

So many wars

Yet if that is the 'already', there should also be a 'not-yet'; is that not so? One question immediately poses itself. If biblical religion is all about peace and peace-making, why, then, is there so much war in the Old and even in the New Testament? That is a fair question. The simple answer is that peace is not the only value in Christianity. Equally important is the value of justice. And there are times that violence may be necessary in order to ensure justice. For many, that is simply a contradiction: violence to the end of a just peace? The apostles identify rulers and magistrates as God's appointees for keeping justice, both to sanction evil-doers and to protect those who would do good (Romans 13:3-4; 1 Peter 2:13-14). Among their responsibilities may be the use of force. The magistrate 'does not bear the sword in vain', Paul tells his readers (Romans 13:4). While the primary task of the civil magistrate is to keep internal peace, a secondary, related purpose is to protect from outside aggressors, which is why the Bible tells us to submit to them, and not resist them (Titus 3:1). It may appear contradictory to contend for peace by violent means, but in a world of fallen people that is sometimes what needs to happen. Most of us would believe that, faced with Nazi aggression and atrocities, there was no other recourse than to go to war against the advancing so-called Third Reich. Other wars are not necessarily so clear-cut. There can be legitimate debate about involvements in certain wars, and foreign policy issues need to be sorted out before deciding on an invasion.

No one who reads the Bible even superficially can

miss the numerous accounts of war. Is God on one side or another? What do we make of biblical authors claiming so? We find the psalmists making appeals against their enemies. 'How long, O God, is the foe to scoff?' asks Asaph, who goes on to plead with God for the destruction of his enemies (Psalm 74:10-11). It won't do simply to say that from a more barbaric ancient time, things evolved into a higher consciousness, so that by the time of Jesus Christ peace, not war, was the ideal. The psalmists were godly people. The outbursts of anger found in several of the Psalms were not from any spirit of barbarity or revenge, as some have claimed, but from their sense of justice, rooted in their covenant relationship with God, the ultimate source of that justice.

An appeal to God for justice is found in the New Testament as well as in the Old. Although it is a parable, the story of the 'persistent widow' is a reminder that the cry for justice is not only an Old Testament one. The widow's request of the judge was, 'Give me justice against my adversary' (Luke 18:3). Because of her persistence, the judge did; Jesus makes the point that God will not delay long over the cries for justice of His people (vv. 7-8; see Revelation 6:9-11). Paul complains of Alexander the coppersmith who had done him great harm, and is comforted by the thought that God will repay him according to his deeds (2 Timothy 4:14). The Book of the Revelation is full of wars and rumors of wars, many of them perpetrated by God the Judge.

Wars in the Bible are not just random violence. There is a carefully articulated understanding of justice which is required by the holiness of God, and which sometimes requires going to war. War in the Old Testament is not *Jihad*. The wars of conquest by Israel were unique. They were specifically commissioned by the Lord in order to provide the promised land, which was a foretaste of heaven. The land was to be a theocracy, based on the principles of divine law. The conquest of Palestine was thus limited and not meant to be repeated. What about the people who lived in that land? They were particularly degenerate according to the record. Israel was called upon to invade the land of Canaan only when the 'iniquity of the Amorites was full' (Genesis 15:16). And even then, Israel did so reluctantly, and never self-righteously. The Lord specified to them that their own virtues had nothing to do with His choice of them as instruments for His judgments (Deuteronomy 7:7-8). The point is, in certain very delimited circumstances, God can and does directly authorize a given war.

JUST WAR
Wars today cannot and should not claim such a divine

approval. The term *just war* may appear to be a contradiction in terms. War brings death, destruction, carnage, and only rarely resolves the problems it set out to solve. After the close of biblical times, when we no longer have God directly telling His people when to conduct a war, is not the chief responsibility of Christians to broker peace? Is it ever right to engage in armed conflict? Have there been examples of just wars? Christians disagree on this question. Yet the position known as 'just war' has come down through the ages as one with authority.

The basic contours of just war are simple.[1] One set of guidelines covers the question, when to go to war. A second set covers just practices within war. When is it right to go to war? There must be a just cause, usually to protect life from unwarranted aggression. The war must be conducted by duly constituted authority, such as the state, and never vigilantes. The war must aim at correcting an injustice and not to provide an excuse for gain. Finally, and somewhat controversially, it must be the last resort. Other means must have been tried before going into war. This is controversial, because it is not always easy to determine how long it is possible to try various solutions before one puts oneself at

---

1. There are a number of useful guides to just war theory. One of the best is James Turner Johnson, *Just War Tradition and the Restraint of War: A Moral and Historical Inquiry* (Princeton: Princeton University Press, 1984).

a disadvantage. What is the just way to conduct an actual war? Acts of war should be directed against enemy combatants, not civilians. There must be proportionality, that is, for the purpose of military advantage, not revenge. Prisoners of war must be treated humanely.

The question now becomes, 'have there been just wars, and to what extent has that justice been nurtured by Christian principles?' A few examples should suffice. While the American President Woodrow Wilson was contemplating a declaration of war against Germany, William Manning, the Rector of Trinity Parish, New York (who would later become the Episcopal Bishop of New York) published the following declaration:

> Our Lord Jesus Christ doesn't stand for peace at any price … Every true American would rather see his country involved in war, if so it must be, than see her flag dishonored or her name stained with disgrace. Every true American would rather see America take up the sword, if she must, than see her bowed down in fear before the infamous and monstrous doctrine that might makes right. Every true American would rather see her country face that issue than see the country untrue to the principles of righteousness and freedom and justice and humanity, for which our fathers fought, and on which our life is built.[2]

---

2. 'Our Country: Address of the Rev. William T. Manning, D.D., Rector of Trinity Parish, New York, Delivered at a Meeting of the New York Local Assembly', *St Andrew's Cross*, vol. 31 no.1,

Manning added a condemnation of pure pacifism, the doctrine that says war is always wrong because violence is always wrong. Having Christian convictions does not preclude justifying a particular war; rather it may require it.

Various wars afford the opportunity to see how a Christian influence has worked a righteous cause. World War II, on the European front, is a clearer case than most since the Nazi movement was bellicose, aggressive, and deceptive. The Nazi goal was pseudo-messianic, that is, an attempt both to purge the world of unfit people and to establish a millennial kingdom, the Third Reich. Much of the ideology was pagan, based on pan-Aryan race theory, a mixture of mythology and pseudo-science that claimed white people were from a purer race than any other group.[3] Certainly, then, there was just cause for the Allies to enter the war. Although some attempts had been made to appease the Germans, that strategy turned out to be massively misguided. Nor was it particularly Christian. 'This morning I had another talk with the German Chancellor, Herr Hitler, and here is the paper which bears his name upon it as well as

---

(October, 1916), p. 31.

3.   Adolph Hitler was known to rely on so-called scientific theories such as Lanz von Liebenfels's doctrine of 'Ariosophy', and Joseph Reimer's idea of a 'Pan-German Germany'.

mine', said Neville Chamberlain, then the British Prime Minister. He added: 'We regard the agreement signed last night and the Anglo-German Naval Agreement, as symbolic of the desire of our two peoples never to go to war with one another again.' It turned out to be an agreement Hitler had no intention of honoring.

When it became clear that the Nazi movement would stop at nothing to gain control of the world, it also became clear that war was the only proper response. Many of the world's leaders, both clergy and political leaders, recognized the essentially pagan nature of the Nazi aggressors. Perhaps the most notable among them was Winston Churchill. His leadership inspired so many allies. We do not know a great deal about his personal faith, yet his worldview was clearly Christian.

At first, standing nearly alone in the opposition to the Nazis, Churchill inspired engagement in the war for reasons of divine providence. He believed God had placed him on earth 'for such a time as this', in order to preserve not only democracy but Christian civilization. According to historian John Lukacs, in the darkest hours of 1940, when it looked as though the German forces could actually prevail, Churchill wrote Roosevelt to say that London was a 'strong City of Refuge which enshrines the title deeds of human progress and is of deep consequence to Christian civilization.'[4] Later in life, he would wistfully wonder what might become of the next generation, 'if God wearied of mankind'.

When Churchill met Franklin D. Roosevelt on H.M.S. Prince of Wales, in order to sign the Atlantic Charter, Churchill proposed singing the hymn, 'Onward Christian Soldiers' together. Although the theme 'marching as to war' is clearly a metaphor for the Christian life, Churchill saw these lines as an inspiration for the group that was gathered. His famous words of explanation were these:

> We sang 'Onward, Christian Soldiers' indeed, and I felt that this was no vain presumption, but that we had the right to feel that we were serving a cause for the sake of which a trumpet has sounded from on high. When I looked upon that densely packed congregation of fighting men of the same language, of the same faith, of the same fundamental laws, of the same ideals ... it swept across me that here was the only hope, but also the sure hope, of saving the world from measureless degradation.[5]

Surely several factors motivated the Allies to go to war against the Nazis. But the Christian influence, resting on just war theory, was one of the strongest. In compliance

---

4. John Lukacs, *Churchill: Visionary, Statesman, Historian* (New Haven, CT: Yale University Press, 2002), p. 95.

5. [http://www.ibiblio.org/pha/timeline/410824awp.html]

with the theory, as well, the post-war magnanimity of the Allies should be admired. Their generous participation in the reconstruction of Germany was not only right but worked out practically to be the very best policy in the end.

RESISTANCE

Thoughtful readers will of course recognize that the church was not uniformly opposed to the Nazi movement, as was already mentioned. The German churches, with some exceptions, were uncritical of the rising Nazi movement. In part this is because there was a certain exhaustion after the end of the First World War. In part, as well, there was an unhealthy relationship between church and state, altar and crown. Besides that, many Christians were tempted by anti-Semitism, often blaming the Jews for some of the failed economic policies of the 1920s. Some made the connection that Karl Marx, the philosopher who inspired communism, was partly Jewish. The same complacency could be found in other countries. France, within and without the church, for example, tended to blame the Jews for its economic woes. Throughout Europe there existed right-wing groups who believed that somehow the Nazis had a point. During the war itself, collaboration with the Germans was not uncommon. Even those who were repulsed by the pagan character of Nazism, such as Bishop Gerlier of Lyon, mentioned earlier, felt that cooperation with the Vichy government, the puppet regime of the Nazis, was best for the safety of France.

These examples of partial or total collaboration on the part of Christians are lamentable. There is no excuse. However understandable are the pressures on the churches to put up little significant resistance, there can be no justification for it, only reparations. And we still have much to learn as we face the future.

Having said this, we should not ignore the many courageous people who did stand against the tide, and whose resistance made a great difference. What does the just war principle of a duly constituted authority mean in an occupied land? World War II presents a number of scenarios where Christian consciousness was active:

> From the beginning of Hitler's regime, the ecumenical Christian movement (its central offices were located in Geneva, London and New York) strongly condemned developments in Nazi Germany that threatened the independence of Christian Churches and the safety of Jews. On May 26 and 29, 1933, twelve hundred American clergymen from 26 different Christian denominations sponsored an advertisement in *The New York Times* condemning anti-Jewish activities in Nazi Germany. Leaders of the Federal Council of Churches (a Protestant group), located in the United States, sent angry letters in 1933 to their colleagues in the German Churches, demanding public statements denouncing Nazi policies. Between 1933 and 1945,

there were six major statements from the leaders of Churches in this country and in Europe (outside the Third Reich) that specifically condemned anti-Semitism and the Nazi persecution of Jews. (Among the officials involved were the Archbishop of Canterbury and Samuel Cavert and Henry Smith Leiper of the Federal Council of Churches in New York.) In November 1938, the three leading Protestant ecumenical organizations in Geneva, Switzerland, issued a statement castigating 'antisemitism in all its forms' and urging governments to permit more Jewish refugees to enter their countries. In the United States in December 1938, the Federal Council of Churches and the U.S. Catholic bishops issued a joint condemnation of Kristallnacht, which had occurred a month earlier. (It was the first Protestant/Catholic joint statement on a social issue in this country.) In December 1942, after reports of genocide began to reach the Allied countries, the Federal Council of Churches passed a resolution protesting the 'virtual massacre' of Europe's Jews. This was followed by similar protests from the Anglican Church in England and a joint statement by Protestant ecumenical leaders and the World Jewish Congress in Geneva. In Great Britain, the Archbishop of Canterbury, William Temple, gave an impassioned speech in March 1943 in the House of Lords, demanding an immediate end to immigration quotas and an increase in Allied aid to countries that offered refuge to Jews.[6]

---

6.   Victoria J. Barnett, 'The Role of the Churches: Compliance and Confrontation', *Dimensions*, vol. 12, no. 2 (1998). Published by Braun Holocaust Institute, Anti-Defamation League. [http://archive.adl.org/braun/dim_14_1_role_church.html] For a fairly

Sadly the Holocaust, the death camps, and the phony medical experiments went on. The actions and appeals of the churches were often not heard. Perhaps, too, they lacked a clearly articulated long-term plan. Sometimes the rank and file members of the churches were often slow to respond to the call of their leaders.

BONHOEFFER

There were courageous voices inside Germany as well. One of the most celebrated is Dietrich Bonhoeffer, the Lutheran pastor and author who participated in a failed plot to assassinate Adolf Hitler. When the Nazis rose to power in January 1933, Bonhoeffer—despite a promising academic career—attacked Hitler and the cult of the *Führer* (leader) in a radio address in February. He was cut off in mid-sentence. In April he asked the churches to resist the persecution of the Jews, making the famous statement: 'The church must not simply bandage the victims under the wheel, but jam the spoke in the wheel itself.'[7] In July

---

balanced approach to the churches' attitudes during the war, see Victoria J. Barnett, *Bystanders: Conscience and Complicity During the Holocaust* (New York: Praeger, 2000).

7. David F. Ford & Rachel Muers, eds, *The Modern Theologians: an Introduction to Christian Theology since 1918* (Hoboken, NJ: Wiley-Blackwell, 2005), p. 38. A number of biographies of Bonhoeffer exist. Among the best is Eberhard Bethge, *Dietrich Bonhoeffer: Theologian, Christian, Man for His Times: A Biography* (rev. ed.), (Minneapolis: Fortress Press, 2000). See also Charles Marsh, *Strange Glory: A Life of Dietrich Bonhoeffer* (New York:

Hitler (illegally) called a church synod and imposed elections. Bonhoeffer fought vigorously for nominees from more independent, non-Nazi representatives. The elections were rigged, and thus a large majority went to Nazi sympathizers. Soon non-Aryans were barred from taking pastoral positions. Bonhoeffer then urged the cessation of pastoral services such as baptisms, weddings, etc., but his colleagues thought it unwise.

In 1934 Bonhoeffer and his minority colleagues formed the *Confessing Church*, and eventually signed the *Barmen Declaration*, penned largely by Karl Barth, then the best-known Protestant theologian in Europe. The heart of the declaration was to reject any submission of the church to the state, and to confess that the church may only submit to the Word of God through the ministry of the Holy Spirit. Bonhoeffer spent some time ministering in London and in the United States. He held a position at the University of Berlin. He created a new theological seminary for the training of the *Confessing Church* ministers in Finkenwalde. Time forbids us exploring the extraordinary discipline and style of life in the seminary. Karl Barth himself was sent back to Switzerland in 1935. Bonhoeffer was disbarred from teaching in Berlin because he was called a 'pacifist and an enemy of the state' by Theodore Heckle, a leader in the so-called

Vintage, 2015).

German Evangelical Church. Then, Bonhoeffer's close friend and colleague Martin Niemöller was arrested.

Bonhoeffer was not simply motivated by a general altruism, nor even a Lutheran cultural tradition. Though he was not a fundamentalist in the strictest sense he had a high view of Scripture and of the relation of sound theology to social action. Perhaps the clearest place where this is apparent is in *Life Together*.[8] Here he affirms the centrality of Christ's person and work in no uncertain terms: 'First, Christians are persons who no longer seek their salvation, their deliverance, their justification in themselves, but in Jesus Christ alone.' He also firmly argued that the Christian community must act in the world, even when that action will mean defying the world's systems.[9]

After being prohibited from publishing his thoughts or even speaking them publicly, Bonhoeffer joined an anti-Hitler military intelligence organization known as the *Abwehr*. He was brought into the organization by his friend Dohnanyi, on the grounds that his contacts could be of great value to Germany, which was meant to protect him from the draft. In fact he

---

8. Dietrich Bonhoeffer, *Life Together*, in Works, vol. 5, Gerhard Ludwig & Albrecht Schönherr, trans. & eds, (Minneapolis: Fortress Press, 2005), pp. 25-118.

9. ibid., 27-31.

made a good many clandestine visits abroad in order to garner support against Hitler. When he learned of the widespread persecution of the Jews he became increasingly convinced that action was needed, not just words. He made the famous remark: 'The ultimate question for a responsible man to ask is not how he is to extricate himself heroically from the affair, but how the coming generation shall continue to live.'[10] He engaged in numerous operations to help Jews escape into Switzerland, which was officially neutral.

On April 5, 1943 Bonhoeffer was arrested, along with Dohnanyi, because of the rivalry between the *Abwehr* and the *SS*, the *Schutzstaffel*, a Nazi pro-Hitler intelligence agency. When, subsequently, the Gestapo discovered several intrigues involving helping Jews escape, Bonhoeffer was imprisoned at the *Tegel* military detention center, awaiting his trial. There he wrote what became *Letters and Papers from Prison*, which were smuggled out of the center. Sympathetic guards even offered him a way to escape, but Bonhoeffer refused, on the grounds that the Nazi reprisals would victimize his family.

A plot by some members of the *Abwehr* on Hitler's

---

10. Dietrich Bonhoeffer, 'After Ten Years', *Letters and Papers from Prison*, ed. Eberhard Bethge, trans. Reginald H. Fuller (New York: Macmillan, 1953), p. 21-2.

life on July 20, 1944 failed. When it was discovered that Bonhoeffer was connected to the conspirators, he was sent to a high security prison camp run by the Gestapo, and then to Buchenwald, and finally to Flossenbürg concentration camp. Hitler ordered the conspirators executed. After a trial without witnesses or documents or any defense, he was condemned and sent to the gallows on April 9, 1945, where he died along with several other conspirators. This was two weeks before the American Army came to liberate the camps. Several in his family were executed as well.

Bonhoeffer accomplished a great deal in his short life. While his group was unsuccessful in the plot to assassinate Hitler, he and his colleagues were nevertheless able to inform a great many people around Europe of the evils of Nazism, which presumably helped to shorten the war. But he has also inspired generations not only by his life's story but by his numerous writings, including classics such as *Life Together* and *The Cost of Discipleship*.

Resistance in Holland

Resistance occurred outside of Germany as well. The Scandinavians and the Dutch were particularly active in protecting the Jews and resisting various Nazi occupation policies. The Germans invaded Holland in 1940. The Queen of the Netherlands fled with her family to Great Britain. A puppet government was set up of Dutch Nazis. During the occupation a number of Dutch people resisted in various ways. There was an underground army which effected significant demolition of Nazi strongholds. One of the leaders of the resistance was the theologian Klaas Schilder (1890-1952). He was a strong critic of the Nazis before and during the occupation. He wrote numerous articles and made public remarks denouncing the paganism of the Nazis. Several articles were published in *De Reformatie*, a weekly Protestant journal of which he was the main editor. For his criticisms he was imprisoned and sent to the German-run camp Arnhem where he was held until December 6, 1940. When released he was told he could not participate in any of his political party's activities, nor could he speak or write against the Third Reich. Should he disobey he would be put on the list to be sent to a concentration camp, as had already happened to several Dutch civil servants. He then went into hiding so that he could continue writing. He emerged when the liberation occurred in 1944.

Worthy of mention here is a darker side to Dutch history. Despite a ruling in the Synod of 1936 to the effect that being a Nazi was incompatible with church membership, nevertheless some eight thousand Dutch Reformed Christians disagreed with the decision and continued as Nazi sympathizers. They included the son and grandson of Abraham Kuyper (the remarkable theologian and politician). Schilder himself was deposed from the church, on August 3, 1944 for a technical theological disagreement, in spite of the impossibility of giving a defense because of his being in hiding. He did emerge and was present at a meeting later that month in the Hague. When the Germans found out they then lifted his arrest warrant, mostly in order to help their public image. In all, however, Schilder was a great force in helping many Dutch people understand what was at stake in Nazi ideology.

Better known to the evangelical world is the work of Corrie Ten Boom. She and her family were Reformed Christians living in Haarlem. During the occupation, in May 1942, a woman came to the door with a suitcase in her hand. She was Jewish. Her husband had been arrested and the Nazis visited her home, making it understood that she and her son were not safe. She had heard that the Ten Booms had already helped her neighbors, another Jewish family. 'In this household, God's people are always welcome,' Corrie explained. She took her in and they fed her kosher food. Eventually the Ten Booms built a secret room within a closet. It became known as 'the hiding place', which was to become the title of her best-selling book after the war.[11] Many Jews and other resisters came for shelter. Food was scarce, but a network of sympathizers provided enough for the refugees, partly through the provision of illegal ration cards for them.

Early in 1944 the Ten Booms were arrested and sent, first to prison, where the father died, then Corrie and her sister Betsie were interned at Ravensbrück, one of the worst death camps in Germany. Betsie died there, in December, declaring just before her death: 'There is no pit so deep that God is not deeper still.' Corrie was released shortly afterwards, due to a clerical error. In *The Hiding Place* she recounts the cruelty of one of the prison guards, then her ability to forgive him and reconcile with him some years later. All but one of the Jews they had harbored survived.

Perhaps the most moving aspect of Corrie's story occurs after she is free from prison and encounters one of her former prison guards. He had become a Christian but bore the heavy burden of having tormented the prisoners. He asked Corrie whether she could forgive him. At first she could not. Then she remembered Jesus' words, that the Father would not forgive an unforgiving disciple. So she prayed for great strength, and God did give her the grace to say, 'I forgive you, brother, with all my heart.'[12]

---

11. Corrie Ten Boom, *The Hiding Place* (Grand Rapids: Baker/ Chosen Books, 1971).

12. From *Guideposts* (Carmel, New York: Guideposts, 1972) [www.

RESISTANCE IN FRANCE

A final two examples of resistance will have to suffice. One could argue that France behaved rather weakly during the Second World War. The French had been badly defeated by the Germans. France was divided in two: occupied France, and the so-called Free Zone, whose government was in Vichy, run by the collaborator Maréchal Pétain and his colleague Laval. Yet that is not the whole story. A number of individuals helped inspire *La Résistance* (the French Resistance which was able to keep hope alive and pave the way for liberation). One of them was Roland de Pury. Born in Switzerland, he became a pastor in Lyon, the same city where Cardinal Gerlier held forth. On July 14th, 1940 de Pury preached a daring sermon entitled 'Thou Shalt Not Steal', in which he denounced Nazism, Maréchal Pétain and French collaboration. He helped draft a famous statement of resistance known as the Theses of Pomeyrol (16-17 September, 1941), a statement of strong opposition to the Nazis and to French collaboration. The de Pury home was a place of refuge for many Jews who were able to be stolen into Switzerland. De Pury was arrested by the Gestapo in 1943 and put into prison. There he was able to write some of the most powerful texts of the French

guideposts.com].

Resistance, writings not unlike Bonhoeffer's *Letters and Papers from Prison*. He was released to Austria and then back to Switzerland. After the war he came right back to Lyon to pursue his work as a pastor and to continue to write.

Perhaps the most poignant account of resistance occurred in a small farming village in the center of France called Le Chambon-sur-Lignon. Le Chambon was in the so-called Free Zone, but distinguished itself by harboring some 5,000 refugees—most of them Jews, many of them children. Most of the citizens of the village were Huguenot (Protestant) Christians whose families had lived there for generations. Well acquainted with persecution, they had natural sympathies for the Jews and went to extraordinary lengths to hide them, including forging documents, integrating the children into the schools and both individuals and families into their homes.

The story of Le Chambon is beautifully told by a survivor who was born there during the war, Pierre Sauvage, the documentary film-maker. In *Weapons of the Spirit* Sauvage returns to Le Chambon with a film crew and interviews the rather astonished people about their dedication and risk-taking. For them, as he found out, this was not heroism, but the most natural thing in the world. After all, one of them told him, 'God says to love him and love your neighbor. My neighbor was in trouble so I did what was necessary.' What is striking in such accounts is the simplicity of their kindness; not wracked with doubt, nor agonizing over the hazards, but disrupting their entire lives, for the love of their neighbor.

Does Christianity really work in a charged context such as World War II and the pressure of Nazi persecution? First, although admittedly this is only a minority, resistance by the likes of Bonhoeffer, Schilder, Ten Boom, and even entire villages, tells us it does. It might be a stretch to attribute the turning of the tide against the Third Reich to a Christian consciousness, yet without it we can scarcely imagine such a good ending. Second, it is safe to say that had the spirit of a just war not been accepted—had many not sensed that civilization, with its biblical roots, was at stake—the ending would have been dark indeed.

2

Peace-Making: A Time to Bind Up

IMPOSSIBLE RECONCILIATIONS IN NICARAGUA

Peace-making also includes reconciliation. We can find numerous examples in history where the major factor in obtaining peace between conflicted parties is the Christian religion. In the fine anthology, *Religion, the Missing Dimension of Statecraft*, various case studies on the post-Cold War peace movements are presented, all of which succeeded, at least in large part, because of the influence of religion.[1] One case in point is Nicaragua's successful plan for the autonomy of its Amerindian population. During the Cold War a conflict occurred between the Soviet-backed Sandinistas and the U.S.-backed Contras. When

---

1. Douglas Johnston & Cynthia Sampson, eds, *Religion, the Missing Dimension of Statecraft* (New York: Oxford University Press, 1995).

the Sandinistas came to power in 1979 they challenged the sovereignty of the coastlands because they didn't understand the Amerindian culture. As a result many native people fled to neighboring countries, particularly Honduras and Costa Rica, from which they organized a resistance against the Sandinista government. Soon they were banned from returning to Nicaragua.

The Amerindians had lived in the East on the Miskito coast for generations. In the nineteenth century they were strongly influenced by Moravian missionaries, so that their identity had become resolutely Protestant Christian. The Soviet-backed Sandinistas were persistent in their attempts to take over Amerindian territory and turn their government into a socialist one. Locals only resisted in an organized way when the government aggressively took over their hospitals and schools. Armed conflict followed, but many Amerindians fled to the neighboring countries. Hopes for resolution, either by the Americans or the Sandinistas, were met with disappointment. Minister of the Interior Tomás Borge, though a Sandinista, was anxious to broker a peace because he believed that autonomy for the Amerindians was a crucial part of the country's tradition regarding freedom. He also hoped such a peace would strengthen the hand of the Sandinista government against the American-backed Contras.

What could be done? Although the story is somewhat involved, what happened next was that in May of 1987 a large group of Christian leaders met in a multi-ethnic assembly just outside the Nicaraguan border in Honduras. They decided to reject American offers for armament. Instead they rallied behind the Amerindian leader, Brooklyn Rivera, and urged him to negotiate with Borge. At first things did not go well. Eventually, in 1988, the Conciliation Commission launched three initiatives in Managua, the capital. Its members, while sympathetic to the East Coast plight, were nevertheless respected by the Sandinistas. Many of them were pastors. Only one was a trained negotiator. Some guests from 'friendly nations' also attended. The rules aimed at fairness and openness to legitimate criticism. Apologies were made. Even President Ortega expressed sorrow for the violence inflicted by the Sandinistas. Every new session opened with prayer and Bible-reading. This was possible because, whether each individual was a professed believer or not, there had long been a culture of faith and community based on Christian principles embedded among the people.

After ups and downs and a few set-backs boundaries were set that were agreeable to each party, and the way was cleared for national elections. Many Amerindians returned to their land. Assessments vary on the overall effectiveness of the Conciliation Commission, but no one denies its central role in bringing about a peaceful coexistence between the different factions. And everyone acknowledges that without its work, conflict and warfare would no doubt have continued.

MIRACLE IN SOUTH AFRICA

A paradox characterizes our next example. Apartheid, the policy of segregating colored people from whites in South Africa, officially began in 1948. But its origins are earlier. Several factors contributed to the policy, including the dispossession of land, cheap labor (known euphemistically as 'the agency' of persons), and, sadly, a theological factor as well. In the nineteenth century the Dutch Reformed Church accommodated to segregation and even allowed for segregated churches, for ostensibly pragmatic reasons. The argument in the Synod of 1857 was that 'weaker brothers' should not be offended by seeing blacks take communion with them. Arguments were used from passages such as Genesis 11, where God confused the languages of the people of Shinar so that they could no longer communicate. A view of the church was developed called 'pluriformity', appealing to the diversity. To be sure, by no means did every Christian subscribe to Apartheid, but it would take a good while to abolish it.

Thus, a remarkable reversal began to occur in 1994. The time had come to dismantle Apartheid and write a new constitution. Despite considerable pressure from many countries and a change of wind theologically, the change did not come easily at all. The hope was to elect a new multi-racial government. At the time there were no fewer than twenty-six political parties in the struggle. Agreement appeared impossible especially so because the two major black parties, the African National Congress (ANC), headed by Nelson Mandela, and the Inkatha Freedom Party (IFP), headed by Mangosuthu Buthelezi, were sworn enemies. It was feared that should the ANC win the election without participation from the IFP, one million people could lose their lives. Many already had. A last-ditch effort to broker an agreement was held. Headed by Dr Henry Kissinger from the United States and Lord Carrington from Great Britain, several meetings of an international mediation team took place. In the end, the report came out that everything was at a standstill, and no solution could be found to prevent the violence.

But then something remarkable happened. Professor Washington Okumu, the Ambassador-at-Large of the Forum for the Restoration of Democracy in Kenya (FORD-Kenya), the only African involved in the negotiations, was recalled by a team of religious leaders to continue the talks. Himself a strong Christian, he persuaded Buthelezi to continue the process, with the guarantee that the government would allow the IFP to participate in the elections. Prayer constantly accompanied the work of the negotiators. A hastily arranged Jesus Peace Rally held in Kings Park Stadium is considered the main turning point, with some thirty thousand participants calling for national repentance and prayer for peace and reconciliation. Although present at the rally, Buthelezi came armed for conflict. Yet he took the draft of a possible solution from Okumu and passed it along to the other key leaders. Again, with much prayer and Okumu's skillful guidance, the leaders reached an agreement. At noon, April 19, the surprise announcement came that the IFP would participate in the elections, to be held one week later.[2] Okumu praised the 'amazing men of God in Mandela, de Klerk (the then president) and Buthelezi.' Buthelezi declared publically that it was the hand of God that allowed for his party's decision to participate in the election.[3]

Not everything has been perfect in South Africa since those heady days. Yet remarkably, the transition to a post-

2. See Donald Rothchild, *Managing Ethnic Conflict in Africa* (Washington, DC: The Brookings Institution, 1997), pp. 207ff.

3. See Alonzo L. McDonald, 'Foreword', in Alan Paton, *Cry the Beloved Country* (Burke, VA, The Trinity Forum, 1996) pp. 8-9. Much of it is based on Michael Cassidy, *A Witness Forever* (London: Hodder & Stoughton, 1995).

apartheid country has gone relatively smoothly. One factor contributing to the peace was the creation of the *Truth and Reconciliation Commission* in 1995. A court-like body whose mission was to restore justice, the Commission heard cases involving human rights abuses, the need for reparations, and a branch dealing with amnesty. Christians have strongly influenced the workings of the Commission. Anglican Archbishop Desmond Tutu was the first Chairman of the Commission. Under his leadership and that of other Christians involved, a stress was laid on avoiding retaliation and promoting forgiveness. Not mindless forgiveness that whitewashes the facts, but real forgiveness, with offended persons confronting the offenders and accepting their apologies and intentions to restore property and honor, where possible.

Here is one testimony from the Archbishop. After discussing the general principle of reconciliation and forgiveness he spoke of his own family, and then of the famous 'Cradock Four', four young men abducted by the Security Branch Police from Port Elizabeth and taken to Cradock, then back to Port Elizabeth in 1985. There they were assaulted, murdered, and their car burned up.

> But the process of forgiveness also requires acknowledgement on the part of the perpetrator that they have committed an offence. I don't like to talk

about my own personal experience of forgiveness, although some of the things people have tried to do to my family are close to what I'd consider unforgivable. I don't talk about these things because I have witnessed so many incredible people who, despite experiencing atrocity and tragedy, have come to a point in their lives where they are able to forgive. Take the Cradock Four, for example. The police ambushed their car, killed them in the most gruesome manner, set their car alight. When, at a TRC hearing, the teenage daughter of one of the victims was asked: would you be able to forgive the people who did this to you and your family? She answered, 'We would like to forgive, but we would just like to know whom to forgive.' How fantastic to see this young girl, still human despite all efforts to dehumanize her.[4]

The Archbishop here recognizes both the need for justice and the grace-given desire to forgive. Here, Christianity is eminently practical, since it is concerned for both.

MUSALAHA IN THE MIDDLE EAST

The work of reconciliation is ongoing. Surely one of the most troubled spots in the world is the Middle East. Prominent among the tensions there is the conflict between Israel and the surrounding Arabic countries. To many observers the clash is intractable. Largely

---

4. See *The Forgiveness Project*, Feature: Desmond Tutu [http://www.theforgivenessproject.com/stories/desmond-tutu].

unknown, but enormously effective is the work of *Musalaha*. The word is Arabic for 'reconciliation'. Here is their stated purpose:

> Musalaha is a non-profit organization that seeks to promote reconciliation between Israelis and Palestinians as demonstrated in the life and teaching of Jesus. We seek to be an encouragement and facilitator of reconciliation, first among Palestinian Christians and Messianic Israelis, and then beyond to our respective communities.[5]

The main inspiration behind Musalaha is Dr Salim Munayer, a Palestinian Christian who believes that believers on both sides, Israeli and Palestinian, have been so caught up in the political process, and so subject to inherited attitudes, that they cannot properly see that a great unity in Christ transcends their cultural differences. Typically, he likes to take small groups and go on retreat in the desert. There, in isolation, the participants learn to talk to each other, to discuss their issues in a safe place.

One of the premises of the work is that, without sweeping issues under the carpet, the process of reconciliation is as important as the results. Dr Munayer knows that the issues will not go away. Nor does he deny that political issues are real and need to be addressed. But he strongly believes that unless the two sides treat each

---

5.   From their website [http://www.musalaha.org/].

other as equals, confronting the issues will be counter-productive. It is much easier to caricature than to discuss. One particular concern of Musalaha is the ignorance of Christians, including Palestinian Christians, about Islam. Even though both groups live side-by-side and speak Arabic, there is little mutual understanding. In addition to desert retreats Musalaha has a number of programs and resources at its disposal.

Many more examples of resistance and reconciliation could be given. To be sure, it is not always the Christian influence that makes the difference. Sometimes that influence is one of many factors. In some cases it is absent altogether. Nevertheless the number of unrecognized efforts by Christians to achieve real and lasting reconciliation is wrongly *forgotten*. Christianity is thus resolutely practical!

PERSON TO PERSON

Alongside these big-picture kinds of reconciliation, or perhaps undergirding them, are the more intimate, interpersonal conflicts. Almost everyone has in their lives people who have offended them, relatives whom they would rather never see again, friends who have become their 'nemesis'.[6] Each situation is different.

---

6. Nemesis was the Greek goddess of retributive justice, often used as a figure for anyone who has the goods on you, or thinks they do, someone you can't seem to shake.

Every type of personal conflict has variants, and cannot be cured by a set of formulas that apply across the board. Yet often there are recurrent patterns. The Christian faith proves itself most practical when its principles are correctly applied to conflict resolution.

We find in the Bible numerous examples of personal conflicts and the best way to approach them. In fact, such conflicts were present in almost every church mentioned in the New Testament. Leaders have opponents (2 Timothy 2:25-6). Occasionally interpersonal conflicts stand in the way of effective ministry. Paul names Euodia and Syntyche as having difficulty 'agreeing in the Lord' despite their effective collaboration with him in spreading the gospel (Philippians 4:2). Persons with grievances against fellow church members in Corinth were going to the public courts in order to prosecute their antagonist (1 Corinthians 6:1-8). Paul counsels them to settle their disputes within the church, because there is much more wisdom there than in the world.[7] The Bible is the most realistic book ever written. Far from painting an ideal world where conflict never occurs, it not only describes conflict but addresses it square on. All human

---

7. No doubt we cannot exclude every case where disputes occur from going to court, particularly when a civil infraction is involved. Still, the ideal is to keep it within the church, whose judges are generally more competent than the civil magistrate.

conflicts stem from our primary conflict with God Himself. Until our enmity with God is resolved there is little hope of resolving human conflicts successfully. Even when we are right with God it is not always easy to work things out with our fellow man. Yet we should be striving to do so all the time. If we cannot get along with our brother or sister, how can we claim to be inhabited with the love of God? (1 John 4:7-12) Paul enjoins us 'if possible, so far as it depends on [us], to live peaceably with all' (Romans 12:18).

A tall order! Can it work? Many ministries aimed at settling disputes are evidence that it can indeed. One of the most outstanding is called Peacemakers.[8] Their stated purpose is: 'Equipping and assisting Christians and their churches to respond to conflict biblically.' Their deepest conviction, which they render quite practical, is that the God who has reconciled the world to Himself can and does reconcile people to each other, both through the power of His grace stemming from the death and resurrection of Jesus Christ. In their years of experience they have amassed both biblical wisdom and many case studies—many successful, some not—of conflict resolution.

---

8. Headquartered in Montana, U.S.A., their team travels all over the world seeking to help with conflict resolution particularly among Christians. [http://www.peacemaker.net/site/c.aqKFLTOBIpH/ b.958123/k.76A8/Peacemaker_Ministries_Home.htm].

One case involves Janet and Larry, who are fellow-teachers in an institution of learning (the names are fictitious, the case is not).[9] Janet came into Larry's classroom after his students had left, and asked for a moment of his time. Though Larry was busy, when Janet announced that the stated purpose of the conversation was to ask his forgiveness, he found the time. Apparently Larry had joked about her and made fun of her in the teachers' lounge, and she lost her temper and lashed out at him. Though taken aback by her transparency, Larry could only manage to say, 'Just forget about it.' To which she answered, 'Forgetting can take a long time. I'd appreciate it if you would say you forgive me.' He could only muster, 'Sure, whatever, I forgive you. Let's just drop it.' Janet had been planning the conversation for a long time and rather anticipated he might try to make light of the whole thing. So she added that she was preparing to go to the other people in the room and admit to them that she was wrong. She then asked whether there was anything else she had done to offend him. He couldn't think of anything.

Not satisfied, Janet persisted. She asked him why he constantly said sarcastic things about her in front of other people. Larry suggested he was only joking. It did

---

9. Ken Sande, *The Peacemaker: A Biblical Guide to Resolving Personal Conflict*, 3rd ed., (Grand Rapids: Baker Books, 2004), pp. 139-42.

not feel like a joke to her. Others, she told him, were avoiding the teachers' lounge just so they couldn't be the brunt of his jokes. Larry did not take that well, blaming them for acting like the 'little pigs' before the 'big bad wolf'. Janet demurred, and told him folks thought he was a hypocrite because he claimed to be a Christian yet did not act like one. This stung. Janet, also a Christian, admitted that she also handled the conflict badly, often resenting Larry in a sinful way. But she had found that God forgave her and she began to mend her hurtful habits. Larry, caught off guard, began to admit he used sarcasm carelessly, and always felt guilty, but couldn't seem to shake the habit. He finally asked her, 'Is there really hope for a jerk like me?' Janet led him to discover the God who can help us control our tongues.

This story has a happy ending. Not all of them do. Ken Sande, the author, explains that nevertheless such conversations are unpleasant, and can be a painful battle of words. He then says: 'Remembering God's mercy toward us, we can approach others in a spirit of love rather than condemnation. And instead of using guilt and shame to force others to change themselves, we can breathe grace by holding out to them the wonderful news that God wants to free them from sin and help them grow to be like his Son.'[10]

---

10. Sande, *The Peacemaker: A Biblical Guide to Resolving Personal Conflict,*, p. 142.

The saddest, and unhappily most common kind of conflict is no doubt within a marriage. As an ordained minister it has been my joy and honor to have performed many marriages. I always conduct several sessions of pre-marital counseling with the couple before we approve the wedding itself. We go over all kinds of ground, including children, money, sex, liturgy, and so forth. At the very beginning I ask the couple, what makes you better together than you were separately? How can you serve God together better than you can as individuals? Sometimes this has not really been thought through. They are just 'in love', and want to 'grow old together'. Marriage is a great joy. But every marriage will come to places where the pressure is increased, trials bear down, and the relationship is strained. At times such as those, it becomes very important to remember why they are together, and why they were drawn to each other in the first place.

When I was in training for pastoral care a man came in for counseling. Let's call him Peter. After some preliminaries the counselor asked him what was wrong. He said it was his wife. Let's call her Mary. They had been married for fifteen years, and he had had enough. The counselor then asked what the problem was. With that Peter brought a large notebook out of his briefcase and placed it on the table. It contained page after page of grievances, all carefully recorded and dated. On one day Mary had forgotten to record a purchase in the check book. On another she had spoken rudely to him. And so it went: late to dinner, forgot to wear a piece of jewelry, spoke sharply to the children, and so on. This log had taken him years to compose. After a brief discussion of these offenses, my wise trainer looked at Peter and said, rather firmly, 'Give me the notebook.' He would not. It was his. It reminded him of all the reasons his wife had transgressed.

Whereupon the counselor told him forcefully that his problem was not any one of these grievances. Not even the sum total of them. His problem was the record book. An astonished Peter protested that all of these misdemeanors had occurred, and he had marked them down scrupulously. Perhaps so, said the counselor, but those are not the problem. 'What is?' Peter then asked. *You*, he was told. The problem is the whole mentality of recording injuries rather than trying to resolve them. After a dramatic tug-of-war, Peter finally consented to 'lend' him the notebook. He put it in a drawer. He then asked Peter to come back with Mary. After initially refusing, he reluctantly consented to bring her in. To make a long story short, the couple came in, and week after week learned to identify their problem and attack it biblically. Today they are very much in love, stronger than ever. This one ended happily.

One approach the counselor used was intriguing, I have used ever since in my own counseling. He made them identify one significant problem between them. Then he told them to sit at opposite ends of a table. He ordered the offended party briefly to state the problem and then stop and listen to the supposed offender's version of things. After listening carefully, the injured person could explain how things looked from their vantage point. Among the rules in the dispute are these: (1) Before explaining why they felt offended, they had to admit some part of the problem themselves (following Jesus' *dictum* to take out the log in your own eye before finding the speck in a brother's eye, Matthew 7:5). (2) No one was allowed to accuse the other in any kind of personal way; they could only address the problem not the person. (3) No more than one problem per week could be addressed. (4) Apologies had to be made, accompanied by intentions to make amends. (5) A next step had to be outlined before they could leave the table. These may seem rather wooden, even mechanical. But my trainer pointed out that sometimes couples struggle so much, they need a mechanical way to begin addressing their problem, or inevitably they would slouch into fights and arguments. The table between the couple signifies the need to be objective, rather than sitting on the couch and holding hands, which tends to make things emotional. In their final session, when things were going quite well, the counselor asked Peter what he should do with the notebook. Peter said he could throw it away. The counselor asked Peter to do that himself, in front of his wife.

The reader may be tempted to think such methods could be conducted by any kind of counselor, Christian or not. Certainly there is common wisdom here and almost anyone could apply the five steps and hope to succeed. What is specifically Christian, though, is the seriousness of the theological background for the true nature of the problem and its solution. Carl Gustav Jung, far more than his rival, Sigmund Freud, recognized the search for meaning behind so many problems his clients brought to him. 'Among all my patients in the second half of life—that is to say over 35—there has not been one whose problem in the last resort was not that of finding a religious outlook to life.'[11] Christian psychologist Richard Winter thoughtfully relates the matter of forgiveness to the Christian worldview. He says there is very little mention of forgiveness in the literature on psychoanalysis in contemporary psychotherapy, even though it is at the heart of Christian relationships. He lists several reasons for this absence, among which is the

---

11. Carl Gustav Jung, *Modern Man in Search of a Soul* (New York: Harcourt, Brace, 1933), p. 229.

shame of admitting the real need for forgiveness. But forgiveness is always available, though the pain and the hurt may last a long time, because Jesus Christ bore our sins in His own body on the cross.[12]

Throughout the sessions my trainer kept reminding the couple that they could not do any of this in their own strength. The kind of love God required, only He could empower. The apostle Paul eloquently describes the contours of love in a well-known passage of Scripture (1 Corinthians 13:4-7):

> Love is patient, love is kind. It does not envy, it does not boast, it is not proud. It does not dishonor others, it is not self-seeking, it is not easily angered, it keeps no record of wrongs. Love does not delight in evil but rejoices with the truth. It always protects, always trusts, always hopes, always perseveres.

Such love is so demanding, so out of reach that only the gospel could break down our selfish hearts and rebuild them for the service of others. Only by receiving Jesus Christ, who Himself exhibited this kind of love for His people perfectly, can we hope to begin to practice it ourselves. And yet, unlike the lofty ideals of romantic love, Christian love is eminently practical, because Christian love does not keep a record of grievances, but

12. Richard Winter, *The Roots of Sorrow: Reflections on Depression and Hope* (Basingstoke: Marshall Pickering, 1986), pp. 175-7.

freely forgives the offense, and moves on to cultivate the friendship, along with a deeper understanding of the nature of Christ's love for us.

3

Social Reform

THE BIBLE AND REFORM

At first glance the Bible appears to be conservative, if not reactionary, on matters of social reform. Paul encourages the escaped slave Onesimus to return to his master, Philemon, encouraging the two to recognize each other's faith. There is no hint that Paul thinks slavery to be morally wrong. At the end of some of his letters Paul tells wives to submit to their husbands and slaves to obey their masters (Ephesians 5:22–6:9; Colossians 3:18-22; Titus 2:9). To the Corinthians he urges believers to 'lead the life that the Lord has assigned', and not seek to change status. He does say that slaves should take the opportunity to become free if it presents itself, but otherwise remain content, knowing that a slave is 'free in the Lord' (1 Corinthians 7:17-24).

Seen this way, the Bible is a conservative book. It enjoins all Christians to submit to authority, whether it be the civil magistrate or the elder of the church (1 Peter 2:13; Hebrews 13:7). Rather than revolution, enduring persecution is the proper Christian alternative to oppression. Yet that is only half the story. The other half is that because of its fundamental principles of impartiality, equality and justice, the Bible is actually a revolutionary book (revolution with a small 'r'). That is why the Bible has been one of the greatest agents for social reform in all history.

Understanding the Bible on social ethics must involve a good deal more than selecting a few texts. As we have already seen the Scripture has much to say about social justice and about treating fellow human beings with dignity because they bear God's image. While one does not find abundant numbers of texts urging the end of slavery, the entire thrust of the Bible is toward the full recognition of human dignity. That reading is what inspired reformers such as William Wilberforce to lead the charge against slavery in the British Empire in the early nineteenth century. That same reading informed those who fought for the end of child labor, the abuse of women, and the scarcity of health care.

While, indeed, the Bible is generally conservative on submission to authority, there are plenty of indications that conscience must be followed even when the civil authorities command immorality. Jesus Himself often defended the oppressed, in disregard for the rules and regulations imposed by the religious leaders of His day. He dignified women of ill repute (Luke 7:37ff.; John 4:17ff). He healed the poor and oppressed (Matthew 11:5). He could also reach out to oppressors. The story of Zacchaeus describes one of the hated tax-gatherers as being summoned by Jesus and having his life turned around. When the Sanhedrin, the council of supreme Jewish authority, ordered the disciples to stop proclaiming the name of Jesus, their answer was: 'Whether it is right in the sight of God to listen to you rather than to God, you must judge, for we cannot but speak of what we have seen and heard' (Acts 4:19-20). The early Christians were willing to be persecuted, even put to death, rather than disobey God's commands.

SLAVERY

Reading the Bible for its 'conservative' message has led some to justify slavery. Seeing that slavery existed in ancient Israel meant they could justify holding slaves in modern times. True enough, in the Old Testament provision was made for the purchase of slaves as long as they were from outside Israel (Leviticus 25:44-6). Yet slaves had both civil and religious rights. A slave could get free after serving for six years. If captured when married, the marriage was honored. Slaves observed the Sabbath. Upon circumcision the male slave could participate in all the religious feasts.[1]

Modern chattel slavery has almost nothing in common with slavery in the ancient world, and particularly in ancient Israel. The first *modern* slave-trade dates back at least to 1444, when a Portuguese ship prepared to land their cargo of 235 African slaves near Lagos, Portugal. From then on the slave trade grew until it reached astonishing proportions in the eighteenth and nineteenth centuries, especially in North America. The trade was based on man-stealing, a practice strongly condemned in Scripture (1 Timothy 1:10). And no civil rights were accorded the slaves. Modern slavery was based increasingly on race, a concept that developed during the Enlightenment.

While the church was slow to see the full evil of modern chattel slavery, when it awakened to it change was relentlessly fought for. The historian G. M. Trevelyan once said that abolition is 'one of the turning points in the history of the world.'

---

1. There were some differences between male and female slaves in the Old Testament. See, 'Slave, Slavery', in *The Zondervan Encyclopedia of the Bible*, Merrill C. Tenney, gen. ed., Moisés Silva, rev. ed., vol. 5 (Grand Rapids: Zondervan, 2009), pp. 533-41.

Undoubtedly one of the most significant episodes in the abolition of slavery occurred in Great Britain at the turn of the nineteenth century. The British had become involved in the slave trade in the sixteenth century, and by the eighteenth much of the economy of the British Empire (as much as 80%) depended on sugar, tobacco, and cotton grown in the New World by slaves. British ships were sold to the French, the Dutch, the Spanish and the Portuguese for their own slave trade. The merchants would bring goods to West Africa in order to purchase slaves, transport them across the Atlantic, and put them to work in the West Indies and other parts of North America in order to grow these products which would be sold not only to Great Britain but around the world. To give some idea of the horrors of the slave trade, it is estimated that in a given year during its heyday some forty thousand men, women and children were carried across the Atlantic Ocean. Close to 20 per cent of them died during the mid-passage, and many more upon arrival. The working conditions on the plantations varied from the horrific to the bearable. Families were separated, and slaves worked in the hot fields under the control of brutal foremen.

The Quaker Christians were the first to campaign against slavery. They wrote numerous tracts and presented petitions to the British Parliament beginning in 1783. Considered somewhat eccentric, the Quakers were not always listened to. But one remarkable person did command the respect of Parliament. Perhaps the greatest social reformer of the last few centuries is William Wilberforce (1759–1833). Independently wealthy, he was rather a decadent young man. In 1780, while still a student at Cambridge University, he became a Member of Parliament. In 1783 he met the Rev. James Ramsay, a ship's surgeon who had witnessed first-hand the atrocities of slavery on the plantations in the Leeward Islands. Ramsay wrote an influential *Essay on the Treatment and Conversion of African Slaves in the British Sugar Colonies* (1784) which had the double effect of raising the concern of the British and angering the slave-owners.

The story has been told a number of times.[2] Sometime around 1785 Wilberforce became an evangelical believer. He associated with 'non-conformists', that is Christians outside of the Anglican Church. His friend and collaborator, Thomas Clarkson, also a believer, had written a prize-winning essay on slavery while at Cambridge. He had been urged by the Quakers to draw a commitment from Wilberforce to work through the Parliament for the abolition of slavery. Another friend, John Newton, was a former slave trader and now an Anglican minister. He urged the young Wilberforce to stay in

---

2. Eric Metaxas, *Amazing Grace: William Wilberforce and the Heroic Campaign to End Slavery* (New York: HarperCollins, 2007). His own writings have also been published. See *A Practical View of Christianity* (Peabody, MA: Henderson, 1996, 2011).

Parliament and continue to fight the cause from within. His greatest friend, William Pitt, the future Prime Minister, also urged him to introduce legislation into Parliament against the slave trade. Wilberforce's diaries record that he resolved to dedicate his life to two major causes. In 1787 the entry reads: 'God Almighty has set before me two great objects, the suppression of the Slave Trade and the Reformation of Manners [an older expression for moral values].'

A group called the Society for Effecting the Abolition of the Slave Trade was organized on May 22, 1787. For the first time Quakers, other non-conformists and Anglicans came together, united against the slave trade. Wilberforce joined the group officially in 1791. This society tirelessly campaigned, wrote, preached, and stirred as much public consciousness as possible. Despite a great deal of opposition, principally from those who recognized the great loss of profits that would occur should slavery end, eventually the tide was changed. An important contribution to the campaign was by the great chinaware maker Josiah Wedgewood. The design of a slave in chains kneeling with hands raised was engraved into a medallion. The inscription, 'Am I Not a Man and a Brother?' spoke louder than many words. The Society tried to influence other European nations committed to the slave trade. They published books by ex-slaves, the most influential of which was Olaudah Equiano's *The Interesting Narrative of the Life of Olaudah Equiano, or Gustavus Vassa, the*

African, published in 1789. Equiano was bought by Michael Pascal of the Royal Navy, and sent to work in the British colony Virginia. He was later able to purchase his freedom. He became an evangelical Christian, strongly influenced by the evangelist George Whitefield. His book described the cruelty of the treatment of slaves in Virginia. It caused a sensation, and helped many British people become aware of the evils of this institution.

The work of the Society is considered the first of its kind, a grass-roots effort for human rights, wherein people from a variety of backgrounds and social classes worked together, without pay, to end social injustices. Despite numerous battles with illness, Wilberforce was able to campaign in Parliament with legislation, powerful speeches, and tireless lobbying, drawing on evidence from various testimonies about the horrible conditions of the mid-passage across the Atlantic, and the wretched ways in which slaves were used.

It is important to underscore the radically *Christian* nature of these campaigns. Wilberforce was soundly converted, in part through his fellow advocate Isaac Milner in 1784. He records that hitherto he had neglected 'a sense of my great sinfulness in having so long neglected the unspeakable mercies of my God and Savior.' The next year he was dissuaded from entering the ministry by William Pitt, who told him, 'Surely the principles as well as the practice of Christianity are simple, and lead us not to meditation only but to action.'[3]

In 1792 slavery was abolished in Great Britain. The hope was to follow this domestic model abroad. The English poet and hymn-writer William Cowper wrote these lines: 'We have no slaves at home—Then why abroad? Slaves cannot breathe in England; if their lungs receive our air, that moment they are free. They touch our country, and their shackles fall. That's noble, and bespeaks a nation proud. And jealous of the blessing, Spread it then, And let it circulate through every vein.'[4] The slave trade throughout the Empire was abolished by an act of Parliament on March 25, 1807. Slavery itself, though unsupported by British law, remained a practice until the Slavery Abolition Act of 1833, voted in three weeks before Wilberforce's death.

The principal arguments advanced by Wilberforce and the other abolitionists were biblical. The trade was morally appalling, and an affront to the dignity of human beings as God's image-bearers. Owners and traders were greedy and avaricious. In a speech to the House of Commons in 1787 Wilberforce said: 'So enormous,

3. William Wilberforce, *Private Papers* (1897 reprinted, Nabu Press, 2013), p. 13.

4. *William Cowper: Selected Poems*, ed. Nick Rhodes (Oxford: Routledge, 2003), p. 84.

so dreadful, so irremediable did the Trade's wickedness appear that my own mind was completely made up for Abolition. Let the consequences be what they would, I from this time determined that I would never rest until I had effected its abolition.' His Christian principles led him not only to fight for abolition but to set up what he called 'true commercial principles', and even some compensation to the owners for the loss incurred. It must be stressed that Wilberforce did not act alone. We have noted the significance of his friendships. We should also note the importance of his networks. Among the most important were the Clapham Group, Anglicans who were members of Holy Trinity Church, on Clapham Common, then a village to the south of London. They shared various convictions but also prayed together and collaborated on various projects. Today we would call them a 'support group', without which some of Wilberforce's energies might not have been what they were. So, while Wilberforce was an extraordinary individual, the power of such networks is almost always present when reformers are successful. It is said, again by Trevelyan, that one result of this kind of collaboration was the strengthening of the British political process.

CIVIL RIGHTS IN NORTH AMERICA

Things went in a different direction in North America.

Despite many attempts by abolitionists to counter slavery, they were unsuccessful. Officially the slave trade was forbidden in most states, and yet a lively black market ensured the smuggling in of slaves in large numbers. Slavery was so entrenched, particularly in the South, that neither the rhetoric of the abolitionists nor the pleas of authors, such as Harriet Beecher Stowe, with her best-selling *Uncle Tom's Cabin* (1852), could convince southerners to give up the practice. A bloody civil war ensued.

Although the Emancipation Proclamation of 1863, and then the terms of surrender by the South at the end of the American Civil War in 1865, spelled out provisions for the full equality of racial minorities, particularly black people, the decades that ensued saw the rise of policies which kept minorities from full participation in society. Three major barriers were erected which ensured segregation and injustice. The first was court-sanctioned segregation based on race. In a case known as *Plessy v. Ferguson* (1896) the United States Supreme Court upheld a State of Louisiana statute requiring separate accommodations on public transportation for people of color. The effect of this decision was to enact the policies based on the doctrine of 'separate but equal', a piece of fiction which kept blacks in ghettos of sorts, including separate schools, separate hospitals, and so on. Second, there was the disenfranchisement of minorities, particularly in the Southern states. Blacks were kept from being registered to vote, or suppressed altogether. Third, acts of private and vigilante violence against black people, including lynching, continued, unimpeded by government or law.

From this time until the 1950s attempts were made at civil rights reforms by groups such as the National Association for the Advancement of Colored People (NAACP). A landmark Supreme Court decision in 1954 had the effect of reversing *Plessy v. Ferguson*. Called *Brown v. Board of Education*, it declared that keeping races separate in matters of education was a violation of the Fourteenth Amendment of the United States Constitution which calls every human being equal. Still, change only occurred slowly. People responded to the decision and others like it by ignoring it. Thus, very little was changed.

At that point the black leadership developed a strategy of non-violent resistance. This led to boycotts, such as the one in Montgomery Alabama, kindled by Rosa Parks's refusal to move to the back of a public bus (1955). The dynamic leader Martin Luther King Jr. (1929–1968) was one of the main organizers of the Southern Christian Leadership Conference in the United States (SCLC). The group aimed to effect the end of segregation, the unjust separation of blacks and whites in the American South. The *Christian* aspect of the Conference was a critical part of the strategy. King's primary inspiration was the Christian faith. He was also impressed with Mahatma Gandhi's teachings on non-violence. An ordained Baptist minister, he was trained in theology and a keen observer of trends and of human nature. King and the SCLC led many different marches. He was often arrested and put into jail. His home was burned down three times. He was stabbed once.

In early April, 1963 King and his colleagues staged a number of sit-ins and marches against racism in Birmingham, Alabama. The local judge ordered the cessation of all such demonstrations. King politely replied that they would not. So he and several colleagues were thrown into a stark jail. He was given a newspaper in which he read a letter from eight white clergy criticizing him for being an outsider and lacking proper patience. In response, King wrote one of the seminal texts of the Civil Rights movement, now known as the 'Letter from Birmingham City Jail'. By disobeying local laws, they were obeying the higher law of God. The major themes of the letter include an appeal to the white clergy to the effect that the cause of equality could be delayed no longer. 'Injustice anywhere is a threat to justice everywhere,' says the letter. Repentance will be called for not only for the hateful words of bad people but for the silence of good people. The letter cites the importance of good motives as well as good actions. King quotes T. S. Eliot to the effect that there is no greater treason than to do the right deed for the wrong reason.[5]

The most memorable civil rights demonstration was the March on Washington for Jobs and Freedom (August 28, 1963). Some 200,000 to 300,000 people participated, blacks and non-blacks alike. The high point was Martin Luther King, Jr., standing before the Lincoln Memorial and delivering one of the greatest speeches of all time. Known now as the 'I Have a Dream' speech, it was the key factor leading to the Civil Rights Act of 1964, which outlawed all forms of racial discrimination and paved the way for the right to vote without any qualification based on race.

What many people do not remember is the difficulty it took to organize this rally. Various factions with differing agendas had to be urged to come and be represented. The somewhat awkward title of 'jobs and freedom' was a rallying point. Christians felt that only with a united witness could they persuade the country. Dr King's speech was full of biblical allusions. They were in the King James Version, used by most evangelicals in the 1960s. Prominent

---

5. A recent annotated edition of the letter is Peter A. Lillback, *Annotations on a Letter that Changed the World from a Birmingham Jail, 04-16-63* (King of Prussia, PA: The Providence Forum Press, 2013).

among them are Amos 5:24: 'But let justice roll down like the waters, and righteousness like an ever-flowing stream'; Isaiah 40:4-5: 'Every valley shall be lifted up, and every mountain and hill be made low…'; Psalm 30:5: 'Weeping may tarry for the night, but joy comes in the morning'; and Galatians 3:28: 'There is neither Jew nor Greek, there is neither slave nor free…'. Like Abraham Lincoln before him, he combined biblical stories such as the exodus with the modern issue of justice and emancipation.

Simply quoting Scripture does not make a speech Christian, any more than the ability to use biblical images makes a movement Bible-based. Indeed, the Civil Rights movement was something of a mixed bag. And yet the Southern Christian Leadership Conference originated in the black churches. The church is the institution that brought enslaved Africans through their suffering, and declared their essential identity as human beings, God's people from whose love nothing could separate them (Romans 8:38-9). Using the name 'Christian' was a deliberate choice, as the organization wanted to stress the spiritual nature of its work from the beginning. Among the principles reflecting these foundations were: (1) The desire for white Southerners to feel involved. Not all Southerners were racist, and the SCLC wanted whites on their board. By dropping the word 'Negro', which was in the original title, whites felt more welcomed. (2) Black Americans were encouraged to seek justice, not revenge. (3) The philosophy of non-violence was to be respected. The SCLC motto was, 'not one hair of one head of one white person shall be harmed.' This last principle was controversial. Later civil rights groups, such as the Black Panthers or the Nation of Islam, did not eschew violence. But the SCLC wanted no one to be able to call them violent, believing, as they did, that Jesus was a non-violent reformer.

After the heyday of the SCLC, other movements helped bring a measure of equality and justice to the American South. And 'although the SCLC has not forgotten its original goals, the focus has shifted to new causes, including health care, job-site safety, and justice in environmental and prison system matters, as well as fair treatment for refugees.'[6] The SCLC's Christian character is still central to its identity. Is Christianity practical? Very much so. The SCLC was undoubtedly called 'for such a time as this' and life after the 1960s for black people, while still full of difficulties, is very different from what it was, thanks in large part to the Christian approach to reform.

---

6.   Elizabeth B. Cooksey, 'Southern Christian Leadership Conference (SCLC)'. *New Georgia Encyclopedia*, 30 August 2013 [http://www. georgiaencyclopedia.org/articles/history-archaeology/southern-christian-leadership-conference-sclc].

4

Health Care

HOSPITALS

A different kind of social reform, but no less important, is health care. The Bible teaches that one of the devastating effects of the fall is disease and disability. While disease may be the result of specific divine judgment for specific sin, often the two are only indirectly related. At times disease is allowed by God to teach us something. In the case of Job, who suffered so greatly, there was a confrontation in the supernatural realm between God and Satan. Satan's challenge was that Job was faithful to God only because God had made him comfortable. When his health was taken away, Job remained faithful, thus encouraging all of the subsequent generations who read the book that carries his name. Disease in the Bible is sometimes attributed to demonic activity. The Bible's promise of a great future, called the New Heavens and New Earth, is to be a place where there is no disease and no sorrow (Revelation 21:3-4; 22:1-3; Isaiah 35).

Whereas we must wait until the resurrection to experience the fullness of health, there is a present reality to healing. One of the great signs of the presence of God's kingdom is the reversal of disease. Jesus is called the 'great physician' (Matthew 9:12). Much of His ministry concerned healing the sick (Matthew 10:1), but the biblical ideal for wellbeing is far deeper than only physical health. The biblical model for health is that of *shalom*, the Hebrew word for peace, wholeness, harmony. While ultimate shalom awaits us in the life hereafter, we may experience it in part in the present. Jesus came therefore not only to heal the sick but to bring peace.

No one would claim that medicine began with an exclusively Christian dynamic. The Greeks, as well as the Romans, the Indians, the ancient Chinese and the Muslims, all had rather remarkable health care developments. The legendary god of medicine, Asclepius, though shrouded in mystery, is credited with introducing medicines and accurate diagnoses for the ill. He is connected with the snake and the pole, still displayed on pharmacies today. Apparently in the healing temples dedicated to Asclepius non-venomous snakes were used in healing rituals. The staff was associated with walking, after an illness was cured. The well-known Hippocratic Oath developed in Greece through the influence of the remarkable physician Hippocrates from the island of Kos during the time of Pericles (460–377 B.C.). He is credited with focusing on diagnosis rather than frenetic experimental remedies. The original oath actually begins with a bow to Asclepius. The Hippocratic tradition strongly advocated respect for patients, including assuring confidentiality and the protection of life. At the same time, supernatural healing was often a part of the Greek approach to health care.

Historians of medicine make the interesting point that marvelous as these innovations were, neither the Greeks nor the Romans were able to build on that foundation and develop modern medicine. This was partly because the world, including human anatomy, was not understood as physically tainted because of the fall, but only somehow accursed.[1] When Christianity took root, all of that changed. A new sense of sin was introduced, matched by selfless compassion rather than appeals to the spirit world.[2] Reflecting biblical emphases, compassion was not an option for believers. The gospel

---

1. See Guenter B. Risse, *Mending Bodies, Saving Souls: A History of Hospitals* (New York: Oxford University Press, 1999), p. 56.
2. ibid., pp. 69ff.

not only proclaimed spiritual salvation but also charity and material assistance to the homeless, the poor and the ill. The church protected orphans and widows, and also victims of earthquakes, fires and epidemics. After the Christian faith was well established, philanthropy was institutionalized, and various establishments for feeding the poor and caring for the sick were established.

During the Middle Ages extraordinary hospitals were created where the sick could be cared for. Among the foremost were the Benedictine monasteries. These were communities of faith based on the principles of Saint Benedict (c. 480–547), who believed Christ was best served in a society of men (later women were added) which could concentrate on all that mattered most, both for personal growth in grace and for outreach. The spirit of St Benedict's Rule is summed up in the two mottos: *pax* ('peace') and *ora et labora* ('pray and work'). The Rule included a provision for those who were ill: 'For these sick brethren let there be assigned a special room and an attendant who is God-fearing, diligent, and solicitous.'[3] Typically a monk or a nun with recognized skills in the healing arts was designated to be the *infirmarus*, or medical practitioner. He or she would have studied plants and herbs, and been familiar

3.   Saint Benedict, *Rule*, 36/55.

with the Greek and Patristic literature on the subject. Although somewhat romanticized, the account of these healing arts presented by Umberto Eco in *The Name of the Rose* gives some idea of the medieval approach to the restoration of health.

Surgery was performed under certain circumstances as well. Practitioners were reluctant to practice incisions and the like, yet certain injuries and complicated wounds might call for such radical measures. As in Roman times wounds were irrigated with wine or vinegar. Bloodletting was not unknown, though the medical manuals found in the monasteries indicate the best ways and the best places to perform it. Bathing was also recommended, not, as in Roman times, for pleasure, but for hygiene.

The routines in these abbeys included two visits per day to the sick, one early in the morning and the other after evening prayers. The minister was expected to talk with patients, confirm the diagnosis, and prescribe diet and medicines (often herbs which he had pounded himself). These medical visits were not, as is so often the case today, purely profane. The religious ceremonies required by the rule included confession, prayers, hymns, discipline, readings, and the sacraments. Special preparations and special times of prayer were practiced for those so seriously ill they were approaching death. Oil was administered. Some brethren stayed alongside the dying patient day and night, reading and praying with them. Questions were entertained about the cause of illness. Could it be a judgment of God? Had there been enough prayer? In any case no exaggerated separation was made between medical arts and spiritual ones.

When churches, cathedral schools and larger institutions began to supplant the monasteries, which, of course, they did not do completely, hospitals were created and maintained by the diocese. *Hôtels-Dieu* were created in the major cities. Literally a 'God-Hostel', these were places of refuge, places of healing and nurturing for the sick and the destitute.

If truth be told Christians did not always act Christianly when faced with diseased persons. Lepers were not always treated as diseased but as pariahs. During the black death, the bubonic plague devastated some twenty million people from the fourteenth century on. Some Christians developed great compassion, while others looked around for someone to blame. Some blamed the Jews. Others blamed Christendom. A rising order known as the Flagellants went around towns bare-backed and beating themselves with whips. In Venice it was thought that air had become polluted with an evil fog or with miasmas. They quarantined ships arriving at the port for weeks to be sure no one had contracted disease through contact with miasmas. They set fires in many places believing that would reverse the pollution.

Some fled from the urban centers. Nevertheless important exceptions were found. Hospitals in Italy run by compassionate Christians took in the victims. The hospital Santa Maria della Consolazione in Laterano (in Rome) had an enlightened physician whose diagnosis of the plague victims and whose equipping of the facility set the standard for many others. Christianity in the Middle Ages, as far as health care was concerned, was practical.

THOMAS SYDENHAM

These institutions did not simply pop into existence. They were inspired by people. History is filled with examples of persons who were motivated to advance the cause of health care because of their Christian faith. Again, we would never claim that only Christians contributed to medicine and health; that would be patently false. But the following testimonies give some idea of the connection between a Christian worldview and particular discoveries.

Thomas Sydenham (1624–1689) has become known as the English Hippocrates. He studied at Magdalen College in Oxford. He interrupted his work there in order to serve in the Parliamentary Army during the Civil War that led to the ascendancy of Cromwell. After finishing in 1648 he was appointed a Fellow at All Souls College. After a stint in Montpellier, France, he returned and passed his medical exams at the College of Physicians, which allowed him to practice in a limited geographical area. He would only earn the M.D. some thirty years later, in 1676, from Cambridge University.

Sydenham was known as being a strong Christian and as having a strong personality. He was an innovator. His first publication was *The Method of Curing Fevers* (1666). He expanded the book several times, adding sections on the plague, and on various technical aspects of diagnosis. He also wrote a series of *Letters*, sent to prominent Cambridge figures including Robert Boyle. Several have become classics, such as one on epidemics and one on venereal diseases. In 1682 he published a treatise on the treatment of smallpox and another on hysteria. One year later he published what some consider to be his masterpiece, a treatise on gout. The next year he published on arthritis and on dropsy. In 1683 he published a landmark work, *The Schedule of Symptoms of the Newly Arriven Fever*. His final work was a manual on pathology and practice. These works were widely republished at home and abroad.

Sydenham's accomplishments were remarkable. He was among the first to diagnose scarlet fever, distinguishing it from measles. He popularized the use of quinine against malaria. He diagnosed iron-deficiency anemia and initiated the use of iron for its cure. He also introduced the use of alcohol tincture of opium. He was known to have a great heart for his patients. He regularly gave credit to God for his most important discoveries. For example, about the alcohol tincture of opium, he said, 'Of all the remedies it has pleased almighty God to give man to relieve his suffering, none is so universal and so efficacious as opium.'[4]

Sydenham, like the Puritans, had a profound sense of medicine as a calling. The medical historian John Brown, recollecting on the field and its pioneers, quotes Sydenham about Sydenham's sense of the health field as a divine vocation:

> It becomes every man who purposes to give himself to the care of others, seriously to consider the four following things: First, that he must one day give an account to the Supreme Judge of all the lives entrusted to his care. Secondly, that all his skill, and knowledge, and energy as they have been given him by God, so they should be exercised for his glory, and the good of mankind, and not for mere gain or ambition. Thirdly, and not more beautifully than truly, let him reflect that he has undertaken the care of no mean creature, for, in order that he may estimate the value, the greatness of the human race, the only begotten Son of God became himself a man, and thus ennobled it with his divine dignity, and far more than this, died to redeem it. And fourthly, that the doctor being himself a mortal

4. R. H. Waring, G. B. Steventon, & Stephen C. Mitchell, eds, *Molecules of Death* (London: Imperial College, 2002), p. 80.

> man, should be diligent and tender in relieving his
> suffering patients, inasmuch as he himself must
> one day be a like sufferer.[5]

This quote is rich with implications. Notice how the care of others is practiced before a watching Lord, the judge of all. The gifts of the physician are all from this same Lord. No patient is a 'mean creature', since all are valuable, the proof being that God's Son was willing to become one of them. The physician should treat others in their pain, knowing that one day he too will suffer. It is a shame that this founder of modern medicine is not better known. He still has much to offer us.

FLORENCE NIGHTINGALE

Florence Nightingale (1820–1910) is considered the founder of modern nursing. She was born into an upper-crust British family. She came into the world when the family was traveling near Florence, Italy, hence her first name. At age eleven they moved home to Lea Hurst in Derbyshire. Her father was an abolitionist and a Unitarian, but it does not appear that Florence had much sympathy for that 'church'. In 1837 she felt sure that God was calling her to serve others. At the time medicine was not considered proper work for a blue-

5. John Brown, *Spare Hours* (Boston: Ticknor & Fields, 1864), p. 152.

blooded young woman. A few years later, however, much to the anger of her mother, she entered the nursing field. She also decided not to marry, despite a few strong suitors. She traveled a great deal, always with a view to learning more about healthcare. While at Thebes she again sensed a special call by God. In a well-known entry to her journal in 1850 she writes: 'God called me in the morning and asked me would I do good for him alone without reputation.'[6] She also had the chance to visit a Lutheran community in Kaiserwerth-am-Rhein, where she observed the way these Christians cared for the sick and the destitute. She wrote a book about her findings.

In 1853 she became superintendent at the Institute for the Care of Sick Gentlewomen in Upper Harley Street, London. She was able to live comfortably due to a generous allowance from her father. But it was no doubt her experience in the Crimean War that defined her particular approach to nursing care. Considered the first modern war (because of extensive use of railroads and modern communications devices), this war lasted nearly four years, from 1853 to 1856. The conflict was between the Russian empire and an alliance of four others, including the British. Thanks to her friendship with Sidney Herbert, the Secretary of War, Nightingale

6. Lynn McDonald, ed., *Florence Nightingale's Theology*, (Waterloo, ON: Wilfrid Laurier University Press, 2002), p. 278.

was able to come to the first-aid sections in the British camp in the Crimean War and help take care of the wounded. She took with her thirty-eight women, including her aunt Mai Smith and fifteen Catholic nuns. What she saw there was quite appalling. Medical supplies were scarce, hygiene was very poor, and infections were not being properly treated. Nightingale wrote a strong letter to the newspaper *The Times* urging more British help. In response the government commissioned a first-rate architect to design a prefabricated hospital which could be shipped over to the Dardanelles. Well managed, it vastly reduced the death rate in that section.

After the war Nightingale went home and was furiously active training others, writing books and raising money. She trained hundreds of nurses in the Liverpool Workhouse infirmary. She became a mentor to the first American nurse, Linda Richards. Born into a Christian family, Richards shared Nightingale's Christian faith and developed a strong compassion for the sick and the dying. She nursed both her father and her husband through their final experiences of life. She directed a new school of nursing in Boston. In 1877 Richards went to England to study nursing, and while training at St Thomas's Hospital and King's College Hospital, she came into contact with Nightingale and was much influenced by her. After returning to the United States, Richards led the way in founding nursing training schools throughout the country, and in addition she helped to found the first program for training nurses in Japan in 1885. She spent five years in Japan as a missionary, teaching both the Bible and nursing practice.

Nightingale's theology was perhaps not altogether orthodox; still, in most ways it was evangelical, that is, she believed in the basic tenets of the Bible as God's Word; God the Creator; Jesus Christ the Son of God who became human in order to die for the sins of His people and to be raised up from the dead to give life to all believers the personal and visible return of Christ to establish a final order at the end of history. She had a strong personal devotion to Jesus Christ. During her life she never left the Church of England, but she could be sharply critical of its apparent indifference to human need. Strongly influenced by the Wesleyans, she believed that true religion would always manifest itself in the active care for anyone in need. (Wesleyans were followers of evangelist John Wesley, who spearheaded the religious awakenings in eighteenth-century Britain and Ireland.) She once told a dying prostitute who thought she might be going to hell, 'Oh, my girl, are you not now more merciful than the God you think you are going to? Yet the real God is far more merciful than any human creature ever was or can ever imagine.'[7]

---

7. Lynn McDonald, ed., *Florence Nightingale on Women, Medicine, Midwifery and Prostitution*, Collected Works of Florence Nightingale, vol. 8 (Waterloo, ON: Wilfrid Laurier University Press, 2005), pp. 48-9.

JONI

We could name many other Christians in health care, people who, motivated by their faith, contributed to human betterment. In the area of surgical practice alone we could cite Ambroise Paré (1510–1590), who stopped the practice of cauterizing to treat wounds. There was Humphrey Davy (1778–1829) and his protégé Michael Faraday (1791–1867), who pioneered modern anesthesia in surgery. And of course, the great Louis Pasteur (1822–1895), the father of microbiology, who developed what became the germ theory of disease. Best known for the treatment of milk and wine to prevent bacterial contamination ('pasteurization'), he contributed greatly to vaccination and the treatment of fevers. He was motivated by his Roman Catholic faith. The list goes on. We could speak of William S. Halsted (1852–1922) who pioneered modern aseptic practices such as wearing rubber gloves for surgery; of William W. Keen (1837–1932), America's first brain surgeon who worked closely with six American Presidents, including Franklin D. Roosevelt; and of many others.

We could also think of the many compassionate leaders who made health care available to the poor and disenfranchised: William Booth, founder of the Salvation Army (1865), which cares, among many others, for prostitutes and unwed mothers; Charles

West (1816–1898), founder of Great Ormond Street Hospital, which met the needs of uncared-for children and reformed nursing care, which had gone downhill since the time of Nightingale and Richards; Thomas Barnardo (1845–1905), who set up several children's homes in East London; and Louis Braille (1836–1906), the blind historian and church organist who pioneered the technique that carries his name to enable the blind to read.[8]

Instead I would like to finish this section with two remarkable and very different heroes. The first is Joni Eareckson Tada. Her story is known to many. Today she is known for her advocacy for the disabled, for her wheelchair distributions, for pro-life advocacy, for her radio ministry and her powerful writings. Joni's work is the result of Christian convictions, but these convictions have been hammered out on the anvil of her own experience. On a summer day in July of 1967 a young girl named 'Joni' (pronounced 'Johnny'—her parents were hoping for a boy, whom they would have named John) went with her sister for a swim in the Chesapeake Bay. She was tall and athletic. In her Christian faith she

---

8. For an enlightening account of the contributions of Christians to medicine, see J. T. Aitken, H. W. C. Fuller, et al., eds, *The Influence of Christians in Medicine* (London: Christian Medical Fellowship, 1984).

had asked God to grant her a closer walk with Him. She lifted herself onto a raft anchored offshore. The water was dark and she couldn't see what was below. She dove off the raft and into the water. It was the last dive she would ever take. Her head hit a rock and her spine snapped. She would be a quadriplegic for life.

Joni spent two years in rehab. She tells her story poignantly in her autobiography, *Joni*, made into a film starring herself.[9] During those agonizing months she struggled with depression, doubt, suicidal tendencies, and anger. The Lord used a number of people in her life to bring her out of a possible state of immobilization to the faith she has today. One key person was Steve Estes, with whom she would later write *A Step Further* about the problem of suffering.[10] Through the patience of nurses and friends she gradually moved out of her despondency and into the service of others. She learned to paint by holding a brush in her mouth. Through modern technology she could write, feed herself, and become mobile. Though her body was a prison, her soul began to move out of disability, by the grace of God.

Eventually, through a depth of suffering most people never experience, Joni, together with her devoted

9. Joni Eareckson, *Joni: An Unforgettable Story* (Grand Rapids: Zondervan, 1976).

10. Revised edition, (Grand Rapids: Zondervan, 1980).

associates, developed the ministry she presently is fully engaged in. Joni and Friends (JAF) is now one of the world's most effective advocates for the disabled. They believe that special honor should be accorded to the weak and challenged. If it were not for the disabled, the world might forget its poverty—some of which is economic, and some of which is spiritual: lacking the resources to flourish as human beings. As Joni puts it, white canes, walkers and wheelchairs are a glaring and obtrusive presence for an insensitive world. Her own wheelchair is a kind of spotlight which, as it were, illuminates right thinking about the nature of the church and the way God works.

JAF has seen a good many results. At home and abroad the team focuses on raising consciousness as well as helping those in need. They travel to parts of the world greatly in need of their outlook. As of 2010 they had distributed over 65,000 wheelchairs all over the world. In the years to come they plan to deliver thousands more. One summer recently they were in Albania delivering wheelchairs to needy disabled people, many of whom had lain in bed for ten or more years. In many countries in the Two-Thirds World the disabled are viewed as outcasts, pawns of the devil or fate, and are despised. JAF counters such a view with the gospel, teaching people that Christ actually lifts up all people, physically able or not, to positions of real honor, whether recognized or not. JAF counts it a proven fact that countries who recognize the dignity of its challenged population tend to be stronger for it.

Joni, together with her husband Ken Tada, is not only an advocate for the disabled but for life itself. She has conducted polemics against champions of assisted suicide or other forms of euthanasia. Her argument is that it is a fearful and degenerate society which will want short-cut solutions to glaring problems such as suffering and injustice. A Christ-like society will do all it can to help its victims, but will not 'play God' and claim the right to euthanize its elderly, its disabled children, or its unborn. Her message also opposes the 'name it and claim it' views of many faith healers around the world. Ironically, she believes, they tend to devalue the disabled, because they have no room for a God whose purposes are broader than making people physically well.

Joni, Ken, and JAF Ministries are concerned for a world which tends to go to extremes. On the one hand many societies do all they can to preserve our biological existence. They go to extreme measures to prolong life, never accepting the reality of evil. On the other hand they refuse to struggle, unwilling to face one day at a time, and so easily succumb to self-pity and escapist solutions such as abortion on demand or euthanasia of the disabled. Human life has often become a commodity. When it is no longer considered 'meaningful' then it can be dispensed with. JAF has a different approach: there are times not to prolong life, when that means placing cruel burdens on the dying and keeping them from death with honor. But it is always the time to fight against wrong and injustice, including prejudice against the challenged population. This is a daily matter, one that aims at long-term victory. It shows 'tough love', with no easy answers, but attributes a positive meaning to pain, because of the stronger, permanent work of grace. The preciousness of life simply cannot be reduced to its cost-effectiveness. JAF Ministries is committed to working in the church, and with families. In the local church their goal is to encourage organizations to further Christian ministry to the disabled community. This involves forming outreach teams and educational coalitions. They also raise funds for the purchase of wheelchairs and other equipment for the disabled. The many family retreats conducted by JAF are making the crucial difference in thousands of lives affected by human suffering.

JAF does not engage in the politics of pity, which tends to disparage the less 'deserving' forms of handicap. Rather, they practice the true politics of compassion, refusing to gloss over sin and cruelty, but pleading for real understanding, real action, and, ultimately, for the grace of God. No one is unimportant, no one is outside of the pale of care. In the great classic *Robinson Crusoe*, Daniel Defoe says at one point: 'Deliverance from sin is far more important than deliverance from suffering.' When *we* say this, it may sound hollow and insensitive. When Joni Tada says it, you begin to believe it is true.

BONO

The story of the rock band U2 is the stuff of legend. The group was founded in 1976 in Dublin, Ireland. They were originally classified as 'post-punk', but gradually added elements from various styles. The four, Bono (Paul David Hewson, vocals and guitar), The Edge (David Howell Evans, guitar, keyboard and vocals), Adam Clayton (bass), and Larry Mullen, Jr. (percussion), were teenagers at the Mount Temple Comprehensive School, a progressive secondary school in Dublin (where Bono also met his wife, Alison Stewart). Talented but not trained, they gradually developed a unique style. At first they were more successful on tour than in recordings. And wildly successful they were, traveling all over the world. Then, with *The Joshua Tree* (1987) they broke into the recording industry with a series of awards and best-sellers. They feared stagnation and so reinvented themselves with the album *Achtung Baby*. Still active by 2009–2011, they went on a world tour which became the highest attended and highest grossing concert tour of all times.

U2's lyrics are generally spiritual, though not overtly evangelical. Three of the four musicians are professing Christians. One important development in their spiritual journey is the stint by Bono, The Edge and Larry Mullen with the 'Shalom Fellowship', a group which made them question whether their music-making was compatible with their Christian commitments. The time with Shalom, a charismatic group, marked them with the challenge to stand for their faith whatever their professional commitments. The musicians left and decided to go on with performing, resolved to stand strongly for Christian principles. The story of U2 and religion has been well told in a couple of books, well worth the read.[11]

To say the least, it was unusual for a group brought up in religion-saturated Ireland, a place which often failed to convey the message that Christianity was relevant to social issues, to discover the Bible and consider

---

11. Greg Garrett, *We Get to Carry Each Other: The Gospel According to U2* (Louisville, KY: Westminster John Knox Press, 2009); Steve Stockman, *Walk On: The Spiritual Journey of U2* (Bel Air, CA: Relevant Books, 2001). See also Peter Williams and Steve Turner, *U2: Rattle & Hum: The Official Book of the U2 Movie: A Journey into the Heartland of Two Americas* (Random House/ Harmony Books, 1988).

Christianity was just that: relevant to social issues. And it was even more unusual for young persons there to have loved the angry music of Punk and fused it with a zeal for Christian justice. But that is exactly what happened. Bono asserted in his first newspaper interview (*Hot Press*, March 1979) that U2 was dealing with 'spiritual questions, ones that few groups ever touch'. He told the *New Musical Express* (June 1981) that the Bible was at the top of the list of his favorite books. Such views were puzzling for many rock journalists, who assumed that there was nothing compatible between the Christian faith and rock music, or that, indeed, rock was hostile to Christian values.[12] Bono especially loves the Psalms, and considers them the 'blues books' of the Bible.[13]

The group went through a number of changes over the decades, but despite such hard-hitting albums as *Achtung Baby* (1991) and *Zooropa* (1993) the musicians claimed they had never abandoned their overall commitment to the Christian faith and to social action. They were simply highlighting the difficulties of life. One journalist wondered if they had left off the more positive Christian message in the album *The Joshua Tree*. Bono asked him whether he had ever read the Old Testament

12. Steve Turner, *Hungry for Heaven: Rock 'n' Roll & the Search for Redemption* (Downers Grove: InterVarsity Press, 1995) p. 176.

13. His commentaries on the Psalms are as refreshing as they are unusual [http://www.atu2.com/news/psalm-like-it-hot.html].

book of Ecclesiastes. Today they are still touring with their message of honest questions and authentic hope.

Bono has proved to be one of the world's most effective health-care reformers. He participated in 'Live Aid' in 1985 and he and his wife Alison were deeply moved and shocked by the health conditions they witnessed in several African countries, resolving that if they had the means they would do what they could about it. Bono and President George W. Bush met in the White House in 2002 to discuss the world-wide HIV/AIDS pandemic. According to *Rolling Stone,* Bono explains the unlikely alliance of a conservative Republican (political party) and a rock star this way: 'It is much easier and hipper for me to be on the barricades with a handkerchief over my nose—it looks better on the resumé of a rock & roll star. But I can do better by just getting into the White House and talking to a man who I believe listens, wants to listen, on these subjects.' President Bush said that Bono aimed to 'achieve what his heart tells him, and that is, nobody, nobody, should be living in poverty and hopelessness in the world.' According to Bono, President Bush went on to compare the AIDS epidemic to 'genocide', implying that nations who turn a deaf ear are complicit.[14] Bono and Bush have gone on tour together urging funds for

---

14. See *Rolling Stone*, March 15, 2002 [http://www.rollingstone.com/music/news/bono-meets-bush-20020315].

countries needing support in the fight against AIDS. According to the personal profile for Bono at TED Talks:

> In 2002, he co-founded DATA (Debt, AIDS, Trade, Africa), which later became the advocacy and campaign organization, ONE. Today ONE has more than 3 million members who pressure politicians around the world to improve policies to empower the poorest. Thanks to these efforts, along with those of partners and grassroots leaders in Africa, these policies have delivered results. For example, eight million people are now on life preserving antiretroviral medications, malarial death rates have been halved in eight target countries, 50 million more children are in school and 5.4 million lives have been saved through vaccines.[15]

Bono has founded a number of advocacy groups. Some of them are quite imaginative. With Bobby Shriver he co-founded Product Red, which encourages companies to feature a particular line within their other products, a percentage of whose profits would go to the Global Fund to Fight AIDS. Many companies, including Apple, Starbucks, Gap and Nike have responded. Another is EDUN, co-founded with his wife Alison. It is a fashion brand which draws its resources from local countries in Africa and beyond. While the company struggled at first,

---

15. TED Talks Personal Profiles [https://www.ted.com/speakers/bono].

today it supports over 8,000 farmers in Uganda alone to move from subsistence to sustainability. Textile work is done locally and profits turn around to help further research as well as health education.

Awarded a knighthood in Great Britain in 2007, he was dubbed a 'Man of Peace' in 2008.[16] Bono continues to be active in response to different disasters, such as the Haiti earthquake.[17] Is Christianity practical? Do these institutions and individuals make a difference? Absolutely!

---

16. Knighthood is an honorary title given by a monarch for special service to the country. The 'Man of Peace' is a title conferred by the World Summit of Nobel Peace Laureates in Rome, to honor persons who have stood for human rights and the causes of peace and justice.

17. TED Talks Personal Profiles [https://www.ted.com/speakers/bono].

5

The Quandary of Unanswered Prayer

We were visiting a remarkable temple in Taipei, Taiwan. Worshipers approached three large statues, bowing and burning vegetables and paper money. The place was filled with incense. People were moving about from one station to another, asking for counsel, and discussing their life's predicament. As we gazed at the scene a woman came over to us, and in excellent English asked if we were Christians. We said we were; we were not quite sure how she knew, but she did. She told us her story. She had been raised in a Christian home, but when as an adult she began to pray for help in several areas, she didn't receive any. She asked to pass an exam. She prayed for a husband. She asked for healing from a particular sickness. Nothing happened. She then wandered into this temple, and began to pray for the same things to the gods represented by so many symbols. And her requests were answered. Thus, she explained, the Christian God is incapable of answering prayer, but the pagan gods are.

We were somewhat at a loss to answer this kindly woman. It sounded hollow and preachy to say, 'God is not a vending machine!' or 'Seek first the kingdom of God!' (Matthew 6:33). What could we tell her? The experience of unanswered prayer is actually a common stumbling block to the Christian faith. Many people make the connection: God didn't heal me, or God didn't provide what I requested, therefore either God doesn't exist or He simply isn't interested in me. It may be helpful to remark that the frustration of unanswered prayer puts us in good company. 'Why, O Lord, do you stand afar off? Why do you hide yourself in times of trouble?' the psalmist asks (Psalm 10:1). Or, more brutally, 'Awake! Why are you sleeping, O Lord? Rouse yourself! Do not reject us forever!' (Psalm 44:23).

PRAYER CHALLENGES

We are commanded to pray. One of the treasures the Lord left to His church is the *Lord's Prayer*, which most Christians know by heart (Matthew 6:9-13; Luke 11:2-4). This prayer centers on the coming of God's kingdom. It asks, 'Thy kingdom come, Thy will be done on earth as it is in heaven' (Matthew 6:10). Practically, the coming of the kingdom means spreading the truth and the grace of God's presence throughout the world. We rightly judge this to include world missions, where preaching the gospel and planting churches are at the center. We should also expect to see concrete results, such as some of the reforms and healings we have described in earlier chapters.

But what is at stake when we do not see these results? What do we do about prayers that go unanswered? After all, 1 John 5:14 tells us that if we ask anything according to His will He shall answer. Jesus told His disciples: 'Whatever you ask in prayer, you will receive, if you have faith' (Matthew 21:22; Mark 11:24). Again, in the Upper Room Discourse, Jesus assures His disciples: 'Whatever you ask in my name, this I will do' (John 14:13-14; 15:7,16; 16:23; see 1 John 3:22). And yet our experience often appears contrary. We pray for the healing of a child and it doesn't happen. We pray for peace in a given conflict and it doesn't occur. We pray for work, for a spouse, and these do not always manifest themselves.

Several considerations should be of help. First, the condition for all prayer is that it be according to His will, and in Christ's name. Stephen Smalley makes some useful remarks in his commentary on 1 John, in the two places where John, one of Jesus' disciples, reflects on our confidence in prayer. 1 John 3:22 says: 'Whatever we ask we receive from him, because we keep his commandments and do what pleases him.' Smalley comments: 'There is nothing mechanical or magical about prayer. For it to be effective, the will of the intercessor needs to be in line with the will of God; and such a conformity of wills is brought about only as the believer lives in Christ.'[1] Thus, prayer is not a push-button matter. It begins with the understanding that our whole way of life is involved.

Second, prayer is not about telling God to come down to our level, but asking Him to lift us up to His. 1 John 5:14-15 declares: 'And this is the confidence that we have toward him, that if we ask anything according to his will he hears us. And if we know that he hears us in whatever we ask, we know that we have the requests that we have asked of him.' Again, Smalley's comment is poignant: 'The fundamental characteristic of all truly Christian intercession is that the will of the person who offers the prayer should coincide with God's will. Prayer is not a battle, but a response; its power consists of lifting our wills to God, not in trying to bring his will down to us.'[2] God hears our prayers in the sense that He listens

---

1. Stephen S. Smalley, *1, 2, 3 John: Word Biblical Commentary*, vol. 51 (Waco, TX: Word Books, 1984), p. 205.

2. ibid., p. 295.

to them and is favorably disposed to them. Nevertheless the larger picture obliges us to recognize that God does not always respond to us in our terms. His will is better than what we might imagine.

Third, prayer certainly involves making specific requests to God. But prayer is also, more deeply, a relationship. When we pray we are talking to our Father. Consider when we have conversations with other people. While not quite the same as talking with God, conversation implies much more than the words used. A conversation with someone means there is a relationship. Our talk will vary with the person being addressed. Conversations are of many kinds: with a friend about athletics, with a police officer who has just flagged us down, with a minister giving pastoral advice, and so forth. God does not change, yet we come to Him in different circumstances and with different concerns: praise, lament, confession, petitions, etc. The point is that while indeed the specific content of our prayers matters, so also does the relationship between the one praying and the one being addressed.

Not what we had hoped for

Certainly at times God answers our prayers in a straightforward way. Francis and Edith Schaeffer, founders of the unique Christian community in

Switzerland, *L'Abri*, had a daughter who was struggling with mathematics at her school. Priscilla had complained that she could never get through her algebra without a tutor. The Schaeffers could not afford one, so they prayed about it. The next day a Czech refugee came to visit and to ask the Schaeffers' advice about his wife's spiritual needs. The man was very grateful. What could he do? He happened to be a math teacher!

Prayer requests do not always have such happy endings. Joni Eareckson Tada, mentioned earlier in regards to health care, tells about going on a tour through the south of England and coming across a monument in the middle of a tiny village. On it were the names of eighteen young men who had perished in battle in World War I. Joni wondered: could they all have been from this tiny place? Her guide explained that British army recruiters had promised these men that if they signed up together they could then serve together. They did, and like some one million Britons they died together in the 'war to end all wars'. Joni writes:

> The village was never the same. Shops were draped in black and curtains were drawn. But families clung to one another, the church was filled, parents huddled together, tears were dried, needs were met, grief was eased, and that little town gained a heart and soul more noble, more courageous than the

greatest capitals on the continent. Despite all the horror and heartache, some good came out of it all.[3]

She then lists some of these good consequences: sacrifices of praise, 'principalities and powers' (ruling authorities; see Ephesians 3:10) looking on, suffering for the benefit of others, the shaming of unbelievers, and the like. She adds that while God knew very well what these people had suffered, He was no mere spectator; He also came down and suffered more than anyone else. 'We open our Bibles and find that God has his reasons for allowing suffering, not just in the larger realm, but in the life of the individual. Learning some of those reasons can make all the difference in the world.'[4]

This story is not meant to teach that there is always a silver lining, nor that death is somehow a good thing. Dying in a war is tragic. However, the story does show how in the midst of evil some good may come. Surely the people of that village prayed all through the war for their sons to be kept out of harm's way, and return home safely. That the men did not come back was tragic in every way. It meant they would never start their own families, and that mothers had suffered the unspeakable pain of

---

3. Joni Eareckson Tada and Stephen Estes, *When God Weeps: Why Our Sufferings Matter to the Almighty* (Grand Rapids: Zondervan, 1997), p. 114.

4. ibid., p. 115.

a child dying before they did. Still, the good that followed shows how God can answer one's prayers in a different direction from the way they were intended. They may have been praying for safety for the combatants, for the speedy arrival of peace, all of which is quite right. If God did not bring those in the way the praying people had hoped, yet a certain amount of redemption occurred, if only because the villagers clung to one another, and found courage to face future adversity together.

While our prayers are sincere, we may make assumptions about what is best for us or for others. Such assumptions may be absolutely right. Many of us have prayed for people stricken with illness, that they may be healed. And we have witnessed numerous cases where the healing has indeed occurred. At our church service we pray regularly for the infirmed. We ask that the Lord would guide the hands of the surgeons, or that He would make the chemotherapy efficacious. Every so often the minister announces that a patient has recovered. And we praise God for the way He answered our prayers. But then, at other times, no recovery occurs. Sometimes the patient dies after a long struggle. We still thank God for the life of our brother or sister, but sometimes we harbor the thought: our prayers were not answered.

What we really should be thinking is that our prayers were not answered in the terms we formulated them.

These terms may be perfectly appropriate. Asking God to heal a friend is always right. When the healing does not occur, another kind of answer was given. By God's providence, taking account of the larger picture, the 'answer' fits His larger plan for the direction of history. The apostle Paul describes a major disappointment in prayer. After becoming a Christian from an orthodox Jewish background he strongly wished his own people would come to Christ. Some did, of course, but not in the numbers he had hoped for. Romans chapters 9 to 11 is a powerful study on God's providential ways, and gives reasons for Paul's unanswered prayer.

KINSMEN ACCORDING TO THE FLESH

Chapter 9 of Romans opens with Paul's complaint. He is in anguish. He is in agony (vv. 1-2). He so longs for his fellow Jews to come to Christ he could wish himself accursed for their sake. Being Israelites, to them belong the heritage of the law, the covenants, the prophets (vv. 3-5). So, then, why do they not respond? Paul raises several possibilities, only to deny them. Has God's word failed, the word that will not 'return to him empty'? (Isaiah 55:11). No, because, as he explains, not all Israelites by birth are the true Israel, that is, true believers in God, from their hearts. He rehearses some Old Testament history and shows that not all who were born into the Abrahamic family were in the true line of believers. Indeed, not all of them were loved by God, he says (vv. 6-13). God is not acting unjustly, since He even uses evil to highlight both His justice and His mercy (vv. 14-18).

In this most difficult passage Paul then explains God's plan of election. Some are chosen and some are not. We cannot in this short space enter into a full discussion of this important doctrine. We should say just a few things, however. First, God is all-powerful. If He were not He would not be God. Everything that comes to pass does so because He has decided it from eternity. Second, and this is most important, God has endowed His creatures with significance and with freedom. Thus when one of His creatures is judged, it is never independent of that creature's deliberate rejection of God. Since God makes Himself known to every creature the responsibility to refuse Him is blameworthy (see Romans 1:18-23). Here in Romans 9 Paul makes the point that the potter has rights over his clay. However, clay in the Bible is often an image for mankind in his weakness, in his fallenness. Thus, God is not arbitrarily saving some and leaving others, He is merciful to some *sinners* who deserve to be sent away from Him, as do all sinners. Why He does not show mercy to all we do not know. It is a mystery. But there is nothing unfair about it, since all deserve judgment. He reminds his readers that even the prophets had foretold a falling away of many Jews (vv. 27-33).

Paul goes on to explain that in part through the unbelief of the Jews the Gentiles were able to be brought in (ch. 10–11). Here is where we find the bigger picture, in the same way as Joni Tada saw it in England. Based on the teachings of Moses, obtaining God's righteousness unto salvation was never a matter of meritorious good works, but of faith (ch. 10). Through the rejection of many in Israel, the doors were opened up for the Gentiles to come in: 'Rather through their trespass salvation has come to the Gentiles.' But the story does not stop there, for then in chapter 11 he adds: 'so as to make Israel jealous' (11:11). Why 'jealous?' Because seeing the Gentiles receive what should have been theirs, many Jews do in the end respond. Paul uses these historical events to prove his larger point, that although everyone is disobedient, yet the way to salvation is not opened to the Jews only, but to anyone who has faith, Jew and Gentile alike. Chapter 11 concludes with one of the most exuberant doxologies in Scripture (that is, with a hymn of praise to God).

Thus, what began as an 'unanswered prayer' ends with praise for God's wisdom. The marvelous nineteenth-century preacher Charles Haddon Spurgeon wrote the following in the devotional book *Faith's Checkbook*. He comments on Jeremiah 33:3, which reads: 'Call to me and I will answer you, and will tell you great and hidden things that you have not known.'

> God encourages us to pray. They tell us that prayer is a pious exercise which has no influence except upon the mind engaged in it. We know better. Our experience gives the lie a thousand times over to this infidel assertion. Here Jehovah, the living God, distinctly promises to answer the prayer of His servant. Let us call upon Him again and admit no doubt upon the question of His hearing us and answering us. He that made the ear, shall He not hear? He that gave parents a love to their children, will He not listen to the cries of His own sons and daughters!
>
> God will answer His pleading people in their anguish. He has wonders in store for them. What they have never seen, heard of, or dreamed of, He will do for them. He will invent new blessings if needful. He will ransack sea and land to feed them: He will send every angel out of heaven to succor them if their distress requires it. He will astound us with His grace and make us feel that it was never before done in this fashion. All He asks of us is that we will call upon Him. He cannot ask less of us. Let us cheerfully render Him our prayers at once.[5]

No doubt one of the most poignant passages in the New Testament about unanswered prayer is from

5. Charles Haddon Spurgeon, *Faith's Checkbook*, 181, June 29. The ancient word 'succor' means 'rescue'.

2 Corinthians 12:7-10, where the apostle Paul discusses the 'thorn in the flesh'. The passage is at the end of his 'fool's speech' (11:1–12:10) where he boasts in his weakness, ironically so, since his spiritual experiences are far more dramatic than those of his putative detractors. But then, lest he be uplifted too much, God gave him a thorn in the flesh. What exactly was the thorn in the flesh? Was it a physical ailment, like a disease? Some think it may have been a speech impediment. Others, a relational issue. Still others think it might have been his enemies known as the 'Judaizers', who were always hounding him. The truth is we just don't know. He calls it 'an angel of Satan', maybe not meaning any kind of possession but the oppression Satan can bring. Maybe it's best we don't know, and that way this passage addresses any kind of trial or tribulation.

So what was to be done? Paul pleaded three times with God. This is right and normal. Whether a trial is sent by God or the result of our own folly, it is good to beg God for mercy. But then, God tells him, 'My grace is sufficient for you.' In every trial that is what comes first: the grace of God. It is a grace that heralds God's power, which is 'made perfect in weakness' (12:9). Now, these are very real trials. The Lord does not take them lightly. Throughout the Bible we are told to cast our cares on Him, for He cares about us (1 Peter 5:7). At the same time, the Lord does not always answer our prayers in the way we expect. He is not only sovereign but also always has something better for us than what we might have thought.

AGONY IN THE GARDEN AND ON THE CROSS

Surely the most dramatic case of unanswered prayer is Jesus' own experience in the Garden of Gethsemane (Matthew 26:36-46; Mark 14:32-42; Luke 22:39-46). He and His disciples are together on the eve of His betrayal and crucifixion. After the Passover meal they head out to the Mount of Olives, to a slope near the bottom so they could watch and pray. Jesus admonishes His followers, telling them to pray so as not to enter into temptation. The word translated 'temptation' is the same one used in the *Lord's Prayer*, where we ask, 'lead us not into temptation' (Matthew 6:13). It has a double, related meaning: help me avoid temptation and spare me the trial. Both meanings apply here, since the disciples would be tempted to deny Jesus (which Peter in fact did), and the trial of their persecution by His enemies loomed. After His own prayer Jesus came back to find them 'sleeping for sorrow' (Luke 22:45). Such a detail makes it clear that only Jesus stays awake and prays, and only His faithfulness could actually save the disciples.

Jesus' own prayer is one of the greatest agony. Knowing what He is about to face, He asks the Father:

'If you are willing, remove this cup from me.' There is nothing mechanical or deterministic about the Christian message. It centers on the crucifixion and resurrection of Christ. But in His humanity Jesus still pleads for the trial to be removed. While crucifixion was one of the worst tortures ever imagined, dying on a cross would be far worse for the Son of God than for an ordinary human. At the climax of His pain He would cry out, 'My God, my God, why have you abandoned me?' The cross meant shame and the abandonment of the Father. The moment was quite literally hellish. So it is no wonder He asks to be spared this distress. Yet His prayer is perfect, because the next phrase is, 'Nevertheless, not my will, but yours be done.'

As we know, the Father did not answer Jesus' prayer for deliverance. On this side of the event, we know why He would not. And surely Jesus knew at the time, although that did not make His prayer any less real. Our salvation was at stake. Only this kind of love, one that would give up the thing most precious, His only Son, could drive him to refuse to answer Him. Of course, after His death the Father raised Him from the dead and made Him King of kings and Lord of lords. So the prayer was not answered as it was formulated, but a greater answer was given, a deliverance indeed, one that brought Him up from the dead and His people along with Him!

And now, Jesus could never be subject to the grave again, nor subject to such a trial.

Because of this prayer, and God's way of answering it, our own prayers are assured of the best possible answers. Jesus here prayed for Himself. But His earthly life's purpose was to ensure our salvation. Indeed He prayed for us and continues to do so. He never ceases to intercede for us. He had already prayed His 'high priestly prayer' recorded in John 17. In that prayer, before His suffering on the cross, Jesus asked the Father to give Him His people for salvation. Now that He is in heaven, seated at the right hand of God, He continues to intercede for His people (Hebrews 7:25). Because of that our own prayers, imperfect though they be, are perfected by Christ's Spirit, who 'helps us in our weakness. For we do not know how to pray as we ought' (Romans 8:26-7). Romans 8 goes on to tell us that 'all things work together for good' for God's people. Notice it does not say 'all things are good', but rather 'all things *work together* for good.' In His marvelous providence the Lord takes all things, whether good or evil, and makes them work together for the good (the French translation is 'concerts' for the good, reminding us of a symphony in which all the parts work together for the success of the whole).

It is sobering to realize that Jesus' death was marked by His anguished question to His own Father: 'My God, my God, why have you forsaken me?' (Matthew 27:46, quoting from Psalm 22:1, which goes on to say, 'I cry by day, but you do not answer.') There is great mystery here. How could the eternal Son of God, the second person of the Trinity, be forsaken by God? We know that Jesus was receiving upon Himself the full extent of God's anger against sin, though He had not committed any sin. He became sin for us so that in Him we might become the righteousness of God (2 Corinthians 5:21). In the end there was victory, however, as Jesus commended His spirit to God, and then, after His rest in the grave, was raised up powerfully to become the great source of life-giving power (Luke 23:46; 2 Peter 1:3).

Jesus' prayer to be spared from His agony, followed by the greater answer from the Father, means we have a way through all of our own agonies. When we fear that our illness will never be healed, we can be assured that indeed it will. Perhaps the healing will be in this life, perhaps not; but certainly it will be in the life to come. When we are unemployed, we can be sure God will provide for us one way or another. If we are longing for a spouse, we need to know that God does not want us to 'be alone' (Genesis 2:18; 1 Corinthians 11:9). He will provide in His own way and in His own time. The ultimate provision is of course our death and passage into heaven itself. Our own death may come sooner or later, but it will come at just the right time.

Once again, we are in good company. Two great men of God, Moses and Elijah, both asked God for death. Moses, overwhelmed with the burden of leading a recalcitrant people any further, asks God to lead them Himself, and to let him die (Numbers 11:15). Elijah, after the dramatic showdown with the prophets of Baal and Asherah at Mount Carmel, is pursued by the evil queen Jezebel; he decides there is no hope for him and he asks for death (1 Kings 19:4). Are these requests legitimate? Though we can sympathize enormously, strictly speaking, they are not. And the Lord does not answer them. For very good reason. It seems dying for them was an escape, rather than in the spirit of the apostle Paul when he says: 'My desire is to be with Christ, for that is far better. But to remain in the flesh is more necessary on your account.' (Philippians 1:23-4) In the case of Moses and Elijah both men had a mission to accomplish, and they needed to be alive to do so. 'The steps of a man are established by the LORD, when he delights in his way.' (Psalm 37:23)

6

Staying the Course

LOST AGAIN?

The question is very real. Once a person is saved, can he or she ever be lost again? Perhaps you are familiar with the story of two evangelists. One is Billy Graham, the other Chuck Templeton. There is a picture in the Billy Graham Center at Wheaton, Illinois, of three young men about to leave from O'Hare Airport in Chicago on their way to a preaching mission in London. One of them is Chuck Templeton, whose autobiography, written years later, is titled, *Farewell to God*.[1]

For over twenty years Templeton was a leader in the churches of Canada and the United States. During

---

1. Charles Templeton, *Farewell to God: My Reasons for Rejecting the Christian Faith* (Toronto, ON: McClelland & Stewart, 1999).

the 1950s he and Billy Graham were among the most flourishing evangelists in North America and abroad, appealing to thousands in their large campaigns. But Templeton began to have serious doubts about the faith. He came to a crisis point in 1957, when he resigned from the ministry. In *Farewell to God* he explains that he could no longer believe in the creation story as narrated in Genesis. He claims to have found racial prejudice in the Bible. He could not accept Jesus' alienation from His family. Prayer ceased to work for him. His ultimate issue was suffering and death. The tone of the book is not vindictive, but sad. He is sorry for all the people who supported him in his ministry who now are deeply disappointed and hurt.

So, what happened? And why such a different outcome from Billy Graham, who went on the rest of his life to preach the gospel and stand for biblical truth? Chuck came from a poor family in Toronto. His father left the family, which then had to struggle by itself. His mother was a strong believer. Chuck became a sports cartoonist for the *Globe and Mail*, Canada's prominent Anglophone newspaper. He led a riotous life, until one night he came home, shaken, sobered, and prayed that God would save him. At the age of nineteen he went into the ministry and became an itinerant evangelist. He and Billy Graham became close friends. Just after World

War II the two worked together in Youth for Christ. Once, right before an evangelistic meeting, Billy leaned over to ask Chuck to pray for him because he was scared! And Chuck was a great encouragement to him then and often thereafter.

Chuck knew bouts with despair. His absentee father was hard for him. He picked up books by skeptics, authors such as Thomas Paine, Bertrand Russell and Voltaire. Full of doubts he enrolled at Princeton Seminary in order to try and clear up his doubts. The opposite occurred. He came to the place where he just could not believe the Christian faith anymore. There were many issues. He told his friend Billy, 'It's simply not possible any longer to believe, for instance, the biblical account of creation.' Billy argued with him for hours, but to no avail. He could not accept a God who would allow evil on such a grand scale as we know it in the world.

Is it possible to be saved, really saved, and then lose your salvation? So many biblical passages tell us the contrary. 1 Peter 1:4-5 declares that the Father of the Lord Jesus Christ has caused us to be born again to a living hope, and 'to an inheritance that is imperishable, undefiled, and unfading, kept in heaven for you, who by God's power are being guarded through faith for a salvation ready to be revealed in the last time.' It would be hard to state the certainty of perseverance in the faith in stronger terms. Unless it is in Paul's words: 'For I am sure that neither death nor life, nor angels nor rulers, nor things present nor things to come, nor powers, nor height nor depth, nor anything else in all creation, will be able to separate us from the love of God in Christ Jesus our Lord' (Romans 8:38-9). Jesus Himself tells us: 'I give them eternal life, and they will never perish, and no one will snatch them out of my hand' (John 10:28).

THE HILL CALLED DIFFICULTY

So, if this is true, then what about someone like Chuck Templeton, and many others, who at first are so connected, but then become disconnected to the Christian faith? There are only two possibilities for what happened to someone who began by professing Christian faith. The first is that while traversing a very dark place, once a believer, always a believer. Nothing, no matter how fierce, can undo the work of Jesus Christ. Christ did not die to open up the possibility of salvation. He died to save. Perseverance to the end does not depend upon our clinging desperately to God's grace in the hopes we won't be snatched away. Rather, God's grace takes hold of us so strongly that though we might try, we cannot be severed from it. Whoever believes in God's son *will not perish* but *will have* eternal life (John 3:16). 'If you confess with your mouth that Jesus is Lord and believe in your heart that God has raised him from the dead, you will be saved' (Romans 10:9). If I am a Christian, then I am so joined to Christ that sin will have no dominion over me (Romans 6:14).

At the same time it is possible for a true Christian to experience the deepest kind of failure. We can think of two persons in the Bible who fell into great darkness. At the height of his reign, David, who should have been out on the battlefield, lusted after another man's wife, Bathsheba, took her in adultery and then had her husband, Uriah, killed in a war (2 Samuel 11–12). The tragedy of this story is underscored because David already had more than enough. God would have given him more, but only in a legitimate way. God accused him of despising His word and doing evil in His sight (2 Samuel 12:9). However, despite such dreadful misadventures, David was not apostate (that is, someone who renounces the faith). He did not finally reject God, nor did God finally reject him. Surely the most poignant prayer of humiliation in the Old Testament is Psalm 51, prayed and composed after his confrontation with Nathan the prophet and the realization of his guilt. 'Have mercy on me, O God, according to your steadfast love,' the prayer begins. 'For I know my transgressions, and my sin is ever before me,' it continues (vv. 1, 3). David went to the lowest place imaginable: adultery, murder and lying. After Uriah was killed, David said to his troops, in effect, that this kind of thing happens in battle. Yet he still was fundamentally a man after God's own heart (1 Samuel 13:14). And God restored him, though there would be consequences, such as a life of embattlement (2 Samuel 12:10-13).

The other person is Peter, Christ's apostle. This follower of Jesus was in the inner circle along with John and James, and would become one of the great leaders of the early church. Peter had special honor in that he at one point correctly identified Jesus as 'the Christ, the Son of the living God' (Matthew 16:16). And yet, on that fateful evening, before the trial and crucifixion, he denied he even knew Him (Matthew 26:69-75). He did so before a little servant woman. He did so vehemently, with oaths and protestations. Denying Christ is described as one of the most heinous acts of treason possible (Matthew 10:33; 2 Timothy 2:12; 2 Peter 2:1). Yet, Peter, too, was restored. In the moving scene where the risen Christ tells His disciples to cast their net into the sea after a fruitless night of fishing, the net is so full they could hardly drag it ashore (John 21:4-19). After breakfast, Jesus turned to Peter and asked him three times whether he loved Him. Three times he answers that he does, the third time with sorrow that he had to be asked so often. Each time, Jesus tells him, 'Feed my sheep.' It is hard to miss the poignancy here. Peter had denied Christ three times. Now, three times he affirmed that he really did love Him, and each time he was given back his apostolic calling: take care of my children. And so, indeed, Peter became the first preacher in the nascent church (Acts 2:14-41).

In John Bunyan's allegorical classic, *Pilgrim's Progress*, there is a scene where Faithful, Christian's friend and associate on the way to the Celestial City, comes to the foot of a hill called 'Difficulty'. There he meets 'Adam the first', who entices him to come stay with him in the Town of Deceit, with all his dainties and his three daughters, the Lust of the Flesh, the Lust of the Eyes and the Pride of Life, all three of whom he could marry. Faithful reports to Christian:

> Why, at first, I felt myself somewhat inclinable to go with the man, for I thought he spake very fair; but looking in his forehead, as I talked with him, I saw there written, *Put off the old man with his deeds*

> Then it came burning hot into my mind, whatever he said, and however he flattered, when he got me home to his House, he would sell me for a slave. So I bid him forbear to talk, for I would not come near the door of his House. Then he reviled me, and told me that he would send such a one after me, that should make my way bitter to my Soul. So I turned to go away from him; but just as I turned myself to

> go thence, I felt him take hold of my flesh and give
> me such a deadly twitch back, that I thought he had
> pulled part of me after himself. This made me cry,
> *O wretched Man!* So I went on my way up the Hill.[2]

Just after this, he meets Moses, who knocks him down several times, because he had been inclined to listen to Adam the first. Moses represents the law, which is incapable of helping anyone who has succumbed to sin. After more adventures, Faithful manages to remember the free grace of the gospel and continue on his way.

Faithful was echoing Paul's experience, recorded in Romans 7 where, though a believer, he finds himself 'captive to the law of sin that dwells in my members' (v. 23). Calling himself a 'wretched man', he turns to God through Jesus Christ his Lord for rescue (v. 25). Christians may, and often do, fall deeply into sin. This may happen for various reasons and may have various consequences, but not perdition. Here is how the *Westminster Confession of Faith* (1646) puts it. After the strongest assertion of the perseverance of the saints, it goes on:

> Nevertheless [believers] may, through the
> temptations of Satan and of the world, the
> prevalency of corruption remaining in them, and
> the neglect of the means of their preservation, fall
> into grievous sins; and for a time continue therein;

---

2. John Bunyan, *Pilgrim's Progress*, par. 374.

> whereby they incur God's displeasure, and grieve
> his Holy Spirit: come to be deprived of some
> measure of their graces and comforts; have their
> hearts hardened, and their consciences wounded;
> hurt and scandalize others, and bring temporal
> judgments upon themselves. (XVII.3)

So, then, even though saved, and secure forever, still, Christians may sin and sin grievously. They may experience God's displeasure and grieve the Holy Spirit by whom they are sealed for the day of redemption (Ephesians 4:30). But they may never be discarded. Here, Christianity is utterly realistic, and utterly practical.

I NEVER KNEW YOU

The second, dreadful, possibility is that despite so many signs of being a believer, the seed never found good soil, the root never took hold, and no real fruit could grow. In the first case, we have a true believer who fell into darkness, but yet was always one of God's people, incapable of being lost again. In this second case, while the outward signs of faith are there, that faith was never real. One of the most sobering passages relative to the subject of apostasy is Hebrews 6:1-12. At the heart of it, we are told: 'For it is impossible to restore again to repentance those who have once been enlightened, who have tasted the heavenly gift, and have shared in the Holy Spirit, and have tasted the goodness of the word of

God and the powers of the age to come, if they then fall away' (vv. 4-6).

What is the meaning of these spiritual experiences for someone who falls away? Some think they are so many superficial or false impressions. The apostate doesn't really know the goodness of God's word, he or she has only 'tasted' it. But that is to downplay the reality behind the words. Just earlier the author had spoken of laying a foundation of repentance from dead works and of faith toward God (6:1). All of these are real. Yet they are not permanent. A person may know all of these experiences and yet still not be born again, nor crucified with Christ. This is rather frightening in a way. Someone such as Chuck Templeton really did experience some of these great blessings, yet without truly belonging to the redeemed community.

The parable of the seed and the sower explains that while the word of God is preached, and often received gladly, it is only when the soil is right that it takes root (Matthew 13:3-9, 18-23). The devil may snatch it up; trials and persecutions may impede any growth, as may the cares of the world. Only when it falls on the good soil, the soil of someone who 'hears the word and understands it', that is, who embraces it by faith, can any lasting fruit be found. The Hebrews passage also alludes to good soil and bad (6:7-8). It also compares falling away to re-crucifying the Son of God, an impossibility. He died and was raised once. You are either a believer or not. God will not provide further and further for you, beyond what He has already done.

While the church of Jesus Christ may have all the right doctrine, all the right programs, great preaching, and so on, it is nevertheless possible that some of its members do not know Jesus as savior. This may not be the fault of the church leaders. In a lengthy series of paragraphs about the nature of the church, the *Second Helvetic Confession* (1566), says this about such deluded members:

> Again, not all that are reckoned in the number of the Church are saints, and living and true members of the Church. For there are many hypocrites, who outwardly hear the Word of God, and publicly receive the sacraments, and seem to pray to God through Christ alone, to confess Christ to be their only righteousness, and to worship God, and to exercise the duties of charity, and for a time to endure with patience in misfortune. And yet they are inwardly destitute of true illumination of the Spirit, of faith and sincerity of heart, and of perseverance to the end. But eventually the character of these men, for the most part, will be disclosed. For the apostle John says: 'They went out from us, but they were not of us; for if they had been of us, they would indeed have continued with us' (I John 2:19). And although while they simulate piety they are not of

> the Church, yet they are considered to be in the Church, just as traitors in a state are numbered among its citizens before they are discovered; and as the tares or darnel and chaff are found among the wheat, and as swellings and tumors are found in a sound body, And therefore the Church of God is rightly compared to a net which catches fish of all kinds, and to a field, in which both wheat and tares are found (Matthew 13:24 ff., 47 ff.).[3]

These are sobering thoughts. In another way of putting the problem, people may have the *gifts* of the Spirit, but not the fruit of the Spirit (see 1 Corinthians 13:1-3 and Galatians 5:22-23). People can cry, 'Lord, Lord', they can even do great things for God, but unless they believe and exhibit that belief by their good works, they are not saved. 'I never knew you,' Jesus will say of such religious show-offs. These thoughts ought to catch our attention. But they are not given in order to scare us to death. They are an invitation to consider where we stand. The author of Hebrews hastens to add: 'Though we speak in this way, yet in your case, beloved, we feel sure of better things—things that belong to salvation' (6:9). The entire book of Hebrews is a powerful affirmation that Jesus Christ is sufficient to save you from any kind of sin or any kind of trial, precisely because He did die once, and now sits at God's right hand in order to give us strength in time

---

3. *Second Helvetic Confession*, XVII.25.

of need (4:16). His sacrifice was absolutely efficacious for your salvation. That is why so many witnesses in the 'hall of fame' have persevered despite the most dire opposition (Hebrews 11).

WHEN REVIVAL COMES

One is tempted to conclude, in the light of these thoughts, that the Christian life is precarious, a matter of touch-and-go. Such might be the case for institutions as well. There is a saying that what begins with a man, becomes a movement, then a machine, then a monument. Not only individuals, but institutions and denominations can begin well and end in decadence. Without naming names, one can certainly think of seminaries or Christian colleges which began vitally and gradually became more tolerant of questionable doctrines, and then eventually pluralistic or liberal. What happened? One is tempted to say it begins with careless or imprecise doctrinal formulations. That can and does happen. When people begin to doubt the foundational truths of the Christian religion, dissolution can certainly occur. But it also can work the other way. When people neglect to nurture their primary relation to God, they tend to want weaker formulations of their beliefs to follow.

The remedy is as spiritual as the cause. Rather than lending more and more care to details of correct doctrinal formulations, and then making sure everyone is on board with every jot and tittle, the place to begin is with our primary relationship with God through Jesus Christ. Among the seven churches addressed in Revelation is the church at Ephesus (Revelation 2:1-7). That church had a wonderful record, was known to the early apostles, and was reputed to resist heresies. And yet it was forgetting its first love. We are not altogether sure what characterized the love they had at first. Perhaps it was fervent worship. Perhaps great loyalty to one another, or generosity to those in need. Whatever the case, the life was diminishing.

What was to be done? 'Remember therefore from where you have fallen; repent, and do the works you did at first' (2:5). Remembering and changing course! These are the key to revival of religion, both for individuals and for populations. In the waning Middle Ages, just before the Protestant Reformation, things looked pretty bleak. Clergy were uneducated, people were superstitious, bishops were tyrannical. And yet through *remembering*, finding the true source, the Holy Scripture, and changing course, practicing faith not meritorious good works, things changed dramatically within a few decades. During the eighteenth-century Enlightenment a wet blanket covered much of European and North American religion. And then, through leaders such as the Wesleys, George Whitefield, Daniel Rowland, William Williams Pantycelyn, and many others, people remembered the gospel and began to practice it.

Such revival goes on today. We know of one denomination in North America which had mostly become liberal and indifferent which, within a few short years, turned around to become a robust evangelical church body. Many churches in the Global South are experiencing revival: in China, in India, in Latin America. The path from man to monument is not inevitable. It can go the other way!

After all, the history of redemption itself is one of massive revival. When Israel slouched into apostasy, meriting and experiencing God's judgment, eventually, when the time was right, the one true Son of Israel, Jesus Christ, came into the world. Through Him comes unparalleled renewal. Even today, when people remember the first principles of the faith, there can be renewal and even reformation. As Paul put it, comparing the work of Christ's heralds to a Roman victory parade:

> But thanks be to God, who in Christ always leads us in triumphal procession, and through us spreads the fragrance of the knowledge of him everywhere. For we are the aroma of Christ to God among those who are being saved and among those who are perishing, to one a fragrance from death to death,

to the other a fragrance from life to life. Who is sufficient for these things? (2 Corinthians 2:14-16)

Is Christianity practical? It is more than that. It is utterly powerful, even in the face of the most dreadful darkness.

7

Persistent Sins:
Temperamental Inclinations

In a book about the Christian faith being practical it is important to underscore the reality of moral habits and comportment. Without becoming introverted, we should explain how spiritual freedom can be threatened and restored. At first this subject may be of more interest to believers than to unbelievers. But it should also demonstrate to those who are outside the faith that character and integrity are just as important as social impact.

Sin, according to the *Westminster Shorter Catechism*, is 'any want of conformity unto, or transgression of, the law of God' (Ans. 14). The biblical text cited in support of this definition is 1 John 3:4: 'Everyone who makes a practice of sinning also practices lawlessness; sin is lawlessness.' Why this emphasis on the law? Basically, because God's law is the expression of His character. Thus to transgress His law is to disobey the Lord God, and therefore to lose fellowship with Him. The ultimate end for the sinner is death—not only temporal death, but eternal death, separation from God forever (Romans 6:23). By the grace of God, at the cost of the passion of His only Son, we have a way back. We can lift the empty hands of faith and receive the free gift of salvation (John 3:16; Romans 3:22-6). Jesus became our substitute, taking our place, dying in our stead (1 Peter 2:24; 3:18).

While Christians have been freed from the guilt of sin, we are not yet sinlessly perfect. The Bible is equally insistent that our transgressions have been forgiven, and that at the same time believers still sin. Indeed, the Bible tells us that to claim not to sin is to deceive ourselves and to make God a liar (1 John 1:8-10). We are free from the realm of sin; sin will have no dominion over us (Romans 6:14). At the same time, sin is still present, and sometimes most insistently so. Paul complains that he is 'sold under sin' (Romans 7:14). He is so beset with sin that he is at odds with himself, and continues to do the evil he does not want (Romans 7:15-20). There is a war within him whereby sin is challenging his more basic self (vv. 21-24). To be sure, Christ will relieve him of this, for which he praises God (v. 25). But the struggle is still there.

How good it is to know both the realism of Scripture, which tells us not to be surprised by the 'plague of plagues' (to use John Flavel's expression), and at the same time the reality of the cure. That it is the apostle Paul who tells us both about the struggle and the victory is of no little encouragement. Let us confidently examine both realities.

The basic character of sin is to be against God. In that sense every sin, small or great, is worthy of condemnation. Nevertheless not every kind of sin is the same. One can judge this by looking at the different punishments in the Bible for breaking the law. Murder, for example, is considered a more heinous sin than theft in the Old Testament. Killing a widow or an orphan is particularly heinous (Psalm 94:6). Leading little ones astray is considered so heinous that it would have been better for the deceiver not to have been born (Matthew 18:6). Any sin can be forgiven, heinous or otherwise. (The unforgiveable 'sin against the Holy Spirit' is the sin of persistent unbelief, and therefore not a particular transgression to be forgiven.) But still, some are more odious than others.

Furthermore, as any honest person knows, some sins are more persistent than others. People struggle with different kinds of sin according to their psychology, their culture, and their patterns of living. Early on after the fall of mankind, evil multiplied and began to take on many forms. As evil settled in, as it were, various patterns could be traced. We have records of cruelty and wickedness from every culture, however far back we go. The history of human cruelty, from the ancients to the moderns, is well-nigh universal. Under various conditions different cultures can become desensitized to evil. That certainly was the case in the Germany between the wars. How the most 'advanced' civilization in the world could become the most murderous is a story often told. Resentment, prejudice, need, scape-goating, all were involved. Similarly such things as suicide missions require considerable conditioning. How could a mother place bombs around herself and her children in the name of jihadic service to Allah?[1] The New Testament alludes to some people whose consciences are 'seared' (1 Timothy 4:2). No doubt demonic elements are involved in some of these evil patterns as well.

The question before us here is whether such besetting sins can be cured? The biblical answer is, yes. However, there is a difference between substantial healing and the perfect cure. We will now look at a number of particular sins and try to show, once again, that indeed Christianity is practical.

---

1. A practice condemned by a majority of moderate Muslims.

ANGER

Several kinds of struggle involve what we might call our temperament. Obviously sin can be found emanating from every part of our personality. There are sins of the intellect, as well as more emotional sins. The category of temperament includes our basic nature and character. Temperamental besetting sins cover some of our most prevalent failings as fallen human beings. Our first candidate is anger. Some people have a 'short fuse'. Of course, there are varieties of anger: frustration, deep-seated resentment, lashing-out, withdrawal, seething, and so forth. Almost everyone has been angry, and at times anger can actually be appropriate. It is a besetting sin, however, when it cannot be easily controlled. Psychologists tend to see anger as a good thing until it gets out of control. For example, Sheila Videbeck describes anger as a normal emotion that involves a strong uncomfortable and emotional response to a perceived provocation.[2]

Interestingly, the Bible, while it describes anger in a quite different way from the psychologists, agrees that it can be a good thing. Paul tells the Ephesians to 'Be angry and do not sin' (4:26). How can he tell Christians to be angry? Because righteous anger is not just a possibility,

---

2. Sheila L. Videbeck, *Psychiatric Mental Health Nursing*, 5th ed (Philadelphia: Lippincott, Williams & Wilkins, 2010), p. 401.

it is a necessity. Righteous anger reflects God's own character. God is angry! His wrath is revealed from heaven against ungodliness (Romans 1:18). The wrath of God comes upon the sons of disobedience, who practice such things as filthiness and crude joking, today considered trivial, but not before a holy God (Ephesians 5:4-6). We tend to think of God as a soft, sweet grandfather in the sky. Nothing of it. Because of His attributes of justice and holiness when looking upon sinful behavior He is an angry God, or, as ancient theology put it, He is a God of wrath. What provokes Him? Injustice. What is He angry against? Evil.

If this connection is true for God, then what about us, His image-bearers? What should provoke us? Injustice, evil. When we learn of an abused child or a greedy bank or an unfaithful husband or racist oppression, our reaction should be ... anger. The attitude that says, 'I mustn't boil over' or 'I shouldn't give in to my rage', while sounding spiritual, is actually quite sub-Christian when righteous anger is called for. This is why Paul can tell us to 'be angry'. He is actually quoting from a psalm here (Psalm 4:4). The Psalms come from deep inside the spiritual lives of the ancient Israelites, and so they are reliable guides for our own. So there are occasions when anger is not only admissible but required. Anyone who stands by, unmoved, when witnessing an unfair business practice or the abuse of migrant workers, and the like, is not a Christian but a Stoic.

But catch the qualifier here. Yes, be angry ... And do not sin! To which Paul adds: 'Do not let the sun go down on your anger' (Ephesians 4:26), adding, 'and give no opportunity to the devil' (v. 27). Anger becomes wrong when it takes control. How many people have let many suns go down but many moons as well, on their anger? Unmanageable anger is a problem for many people, Christians and non-Christians alike. Some societies have centers for anger management. There one learns all kinds of techniques such as holding the tongue, walking away, and so forth. An article on the website of the American Psychological Association recommends three techniques: expressing, suppressing, and calming.[3] Expressing your anger is 'assertive', it says, not 'aggressive'. One must simply make one's needs known without being 'pushy'. Suppressing anger is in order to 'convert' or 'redirect' it into more constructive behavior. But this must not lead to unexpressed anger, since that can come back to bite one. At the same time one must calm down by controlling both one's outward behavior and one's internal responses. Just wait until the anger subsides.

---

3.   [http://www.apa.org/topics/anger/control.aspx?item=2]

Some of this counsel is helpful, to a point. But notice how very different Paul's counsel to the Ephesians is. The entire paragraph (vv. 25-32) is a practical outworking of what came before. Paul has been telling the readers how, now that they are in Christ, they have new life, and no longer need to *walk* in the way of the unbelievers (v. 17). Believers have *put off* the old self and *put on* the new self. They are now being renewed into God's likeness (vv. 22-24). He then says, 'Therefore, having put away falsehood ...' and proceeds to give examples. One is to speak the truth (v. 25). The next is to be angry but not sin (v. 28). Then the thief must stop stealing but work with his hands in order to become generous to those in need (vv. 27-8). And the list goes on. Anger-management techniques miss the most important factor in properly handling the emotion of anger: the power of God's grace through Jesus Christ. Being new persons in Christ, while it does not lead to perfection, is the proper way to walk as Christians, which includes handling anger.

Uncontrolled anger is a serious problem. The Bible is most realistic about the reality of this emotion gone unchecked. Moses, the great man of God, the most significant leader in the Old Testament, was prevented from going into the Promised Land because he did not fully trust in God's provision, and twice struck the rock he had been told simply to address verbally. His words were addressed instead to the people, words that were not fully respectful of God (Numbers 20:11-12). Paul himself admits being covetous, which is surely one of the factors leading him to his overzealous fight for 'truth', as he persecuted the church. He tells his readers in Romans 7:7 that he had not been aware of his jealous heart until the tenth commandment, 'You shall not covet', came bearing down on him. It is possible that his awakening to this sin came as he listened to the eloquent Stephen, the first Christian martyr (Acts 8:1). Both Moses and Paul, and anyone else struggling with uncontrolled resentment, were forgiven, and readjusted their lives.

When I was in youth work I encountered a number of cases of young people prone to anger. While in most cases there was temperament involved, a predisposition to anger, there usually were secondary causes as well. One young man I remember grew up with divorced parents. He was furious with them for the effects he believed the divorce had on him. He saw them competing for his attention, not providing the kind of tranquility he imagined normal parents did, and generally embarrassing him. He vented his wrath on other people, particularly adults, but also on his peers. When he came to one of our summer camps he became a Christian. He was now a new man, walking in faith. Yet his anger often still got the better of him. Eventually, with a great deal of love and patient counseling by the leaders, and by constant prayer for grace, he was more and more able to control his anger. At the urging of one counselor he went and met with both parents, and asked their forgiveness for his having used their divorce as an excuse to blow his fuse all the time. He had to do this in such a way as not to drive them to deeper guilt than they already had. Today as an adult, while there are still the occasional bouts with anger, he is a more cheerful, balanced person.

Is Christianity practical with the besetting sin of anger? Yes, indeed. The same can be said of any number of other sins of the emotions. Fear, depression, shame, and many others are both real and curable. While each one is different and requires special understanding, the basic answer for their management is the same: through the power of the gospel, because we are new persons, walking with Christ, we may move from being enslaved by these emotions to controlling them, and redirecting them for more fruitful purposes.

Fear

Another besetting sin of the emotions is fear. Similar to anger, fear is often a quite proper human emotion. Appropriate fear is rooted in deference or respect. Such a human quality still might derive from God, whose image we bear. Although strictly speaking God owes no one deference or respect, one might be able to argue that within the Holy Trinity there is something like mutual respect and perhaps even the unique respect of the Son for the Father, and of the Spirit for the Father and the Son. And, certainly, when the Son became incarnate as a human being, in His role as savior, He did everything in respectful obedience to the Father (John 7:16; 8:28; 17:4).

Throughout Scripture, a proper fear of the Lord is enjoined (Leviticus 19:14,32; 25:17; Psalm 2:11; 15:4; 19:9; 34:7,9,11; Jeremiah 5:24). Proper fear of God is not dread or terror. The main meaning of 'fearing the Lord' is trust (Psalm 40:3; 115:11; Hosea 3:5). Having said that, fearing the Lord is not simply a matter of confidence. There is a proper sense of awe that should characterize our trust, because of who God is (Deuteronomy 4:24; Hebrews 12:29). Still, proper fear of the Lord is in contrast to the unhealthy fear in those who cannot help us (Isaiah 8:13; 41:13; Acts 9:31). God is there to save us and bring us into His sheepfold. Such fear incites us to persuade others of the truth of the gospel (2 Corinthians 5:11).

By contrast to this right kind of fear, sinful fear is an unhealthy dread. We may fear another person. While respect for mother and father is proper (Exodus 20:12; Matthew 15:4; Ephesians 6:2), a child should never be terrified by his or her parents. What can and does happen is an abusive father or a controlling mother driving the dread of them into their children, a dread that can become a besetting sin. Sometimes another person is hard to face because we fear their presence. Perhaps they know something about us that we would rather forget. Perhaps we have offended that person or lied to him, and facing him means feeling exposed. In the play, made into a movie, *One Flew Over the Cuckoo's Nest*, the head nurse of a mental institution for recidivists, Mildred Ratched, uses various techniques of humiliation as well as medicines to drive her patients into a codependent dread of her. One of her victims, Billy Bibbit, stutters and loses whatever confidence he had developed when she confronts him. The fanciful ending, a perverted sort of victory, has one of the patients, Chief Bromden, smother to death one of Ratched's permanently damaged victims, and then rip the dreaded hydrotherapy console up off the floor, throw it through a window and escape, to the cheers of the inmates. But the methods of control by the authorities in the institution and the slavery of the fearful inmates are insightful, if disturbing.

Besides persons, we may also fear circumstances or even certain rooms in a house. My wife and I know of one person, an adult, who cannot sleep without a nightlight on in the room, or the bathroom next door. In her particular case, her parents used to keep secrets from her, thinking it best that she not know certain things. The reverse was the effect; she developed deep suspicions of the unknown. Darkness became her greatest threat. Nighttime was a constant peril for her. The nightlight helped but did not cure her problem.

Can there be any victory over this kind of slavish fear? Is Christianity practical, and powerful enough to release people wracked by fear? Certainly. However, various considerations must be made if a treatment is to be found. First, the fearful person must be shown that God, and only God is in control of our universe. Not a bare-bones manipulation of whatever comes to pass, but a definitive provision for our greatest need, the forgiveness of sins. John's first letter is a study in assurance. The author tells his readers that 'there is no fear in love, but perfect love casts out fear' (1 John 4:18). What does he mean by this? The wider context tells us. John is concerned that Christians not dread the day of judgment. He explains that fear has to do with punishment. But God, because of His love, has dealt with the guilt of our sin, and so we may stand confident and not yield to fear. If we still fear after believing in Christ, we are saying, in effect, God is unjustly proffering double-jeopardy. It is in this sense that 'whenever our heart condemns us, God is greater than our heart ... for he who is in you is greater than he who is in the world' (3:20; 4:4).

Thus, John is telling us, fear is connected to judgment or condemnation. There is plenty to worry about in the world. Terrorism, crime, floods, earthquakes, airplane crashes ... All of them can and will occur. But the only thing really to worry about is the judgment. If we are accepted by God, then dangerous as all those other threats may be, they are unimportant in the scheme of things. Is someone afraid of the dark basically worried about the judgment? The connection may be quite indirect, but it is there just the same. Darkness may suggest to them 'outer darkness', or being cast out of God's presence. The plausibility of that fear is undeniable. Darkness suggests threats of all kinds. The Bible often associates darkness with evil. Jesus talked about the 'power of darkness' (Luke 22:53). Paul explains that we live in a cosmic battle: 'For we do not wrestle against flesh and blood, but against the rulers, against the authorities, against the cosmic powers over this present darkness ...' (Ephesians 6:12).

But now, we are told, the Father has 'delivered us from the domain of darkness and transferred us to the kingdom of his beloved Son, in whom we have redemption, the forgiveness of sins' (Colossians 1:13-14). Someone who is afraid of the dark has not fully grasped this gospel truth. The reformer Martin Luther struggled with this kind of assurance. The story goes that once, when he was studying for a lecture in the Wartburg, he could 'hear' the devil whispering to him what a bad sinner he was. When Luther came to himself he spoke to Satan and said, yes, in effect, those are my sins, and here are a few more you did not mention, whereupon he threw an ink bottle at him, telling him the Word of God had declared him acquitted and that he had no right to say the contrary. While this story has not been verified, the principle surely is true. When accused of one's sins, one needs to do two things: first admit the accusations are true, if too light; and second, 'remind the devil' that the Bible tells us our sins have been dealt with once and for all.

Does that mean they simply need more preaching about forgiveness, about their safety before the judgment because of Christ's work? Such reminders will not hurt. But they need to be accompanied with practical measures. So, second, when people are truly beset with such fear, it won't be enough to simply preach at them. If they fear the dark, then there is nothing shameful about a nightlight. If they worry about being alone in the house, be sure they have proper locks, and maybe an alarm system. Or get a dog.

If a person fears someone else (their 'Nemesis' as is sometimes said), the best thing is to go and meet with them and try to have it out. Avoiding the person almost never takes away the fear. One friend of mine—let's call him Sam—struggled seriously with his father. Their relationship had never been an easy one. Sam always felt his father condemned him. Some things were small, such as the dad being critical of his haircut or his dress style. Others were more substantive, such as the Sam's choice of friends, or the job he picked. He just never seemed to be able to do anything right. Finally, one day the son decided he had to face his father and come clean with him about these things. The meeting was tense. Sam tried to tell his father that he was right, in part. But he also asked his dad to back down and give him some space. They had several subsequent meetings. Today, while things are still edgy, Sam has a clear conscience and is able to cope with his life.

Things do not always work out so well. Sometimes besetting fear is so deep-seated that therapy is called for. A person riveted by fear is often not able, rationally, to simply listen to good practical advice and go and be different. Fear, after all, is irrational. Often a fearful person will never, in this life, fully overcome those fears. He may go for weeks or months without worries, and then, by surprise, a fearful reminder rears its head, and he is plunged back into the besetting sin. What should he do? Pick up the pieces and remember the gospel. It helps a great deal to know that Jesus Himself was threatened by fear, the fear of abandonment.

At the very end of His upper room discourses with the disciples, on the eve of His passion, He told them this: 'Behold, the hour is coming, indeed it has come, when you will be scattered, each to his own home, and will leave me alone. Yet I am not alone, for the Father is with me. I have said these things to you, that you may have peace. In the world you will have tribulation. But take heart; I have overcome the world' (John 16:32-3). More powerful words have never been spoken. Jesus would be abandoned by His Father on the cross, and would exclaim, 'My God, my God, why have you forsaken me?' (Matthew 27:46). But while He was judged for our sins, not for His own, yet in the end God never abandoned Him. He would not remain alone. And because of that, neither will we be left alone. Whatever the forces that would threaten us and want us alone, Christ has overcome them. So we have peace.

LUST FOR POWER

Joseph Stalin (1878–1953) will go down in history as one of the most driven seekers of power the world will ever know. He became General Secretary of the Communist Party in Russia in 1922. After the death of Lenin, in 1924, he expanded his role and consolidated his power by eliminating all opposition. In 1941 he established the position of Premier of the Soviet Union, a position he occupied for the rest of his life. Stalin is credited with moving Russia from an agrarian to an industrial society. However, he accomplished this by using the most brutal tactics. He imprisoned millions of people into the infamous gulags, the so-called 'Soviet Correctional Labor Camps'. Hundreds of thousands who supposedly did not cooperate were deported to the far reaches of Siberia. His strategies provoked the great Soviet famine of 1932-3 and the Ukrainian famine. The total number of deaths resulting from his policies is estimated as close to 10 million people.

In the late 1930s Stalin initiated the 'Great Purge', in which hundreds of thousands of so-called enemies of the state were executed. They included the major leaders in the communist party as well as the Red Army. His philosophy included the idea of the 'aggravation of the class in the struggle for socialism', which meant he could justify political repression in the name of progress. After World War II Soviet people began to hope that their lot might improve. Rather than provide for such improvement Stalin decided that their hopes were dangerous, because their aspirations could lead to rebellion. So he instituted harsher measures of repression against those who were attracted by ideas such as 'American democracy'. Stalin waged a campaign in the press against the decadent West. He disowned his two sons. In his old age he turned his ire against the Jews. He died alone and miserable. According to his daughter, Svetlana, his death was pure agony. 'At the last moment he suddenly opened his eyes. It was a horrible look—either mad, or angry and full of fear of death ... Suddenly he raised his left hand and sort of either pointed up somewhere, or shook his finger at us all.'[4] Svetlana denounced her father's methods and the communist philosophy. She died in 2011 after living thirty happy years in America.

What drives someone to crave such power? Philosophical convictions alone do not explain it. Many people believe in certain ideologies without the kind of paranoia exhibited by Stalin. Of course, one of the most central characteristics of human rebellion is its desire to usurp God's authority and establish its own. Authority is another word for power. Pride is perhaps the most capital of vices, because it imagines everything to center around us. C. S. Lewis brings us helpful insights into the nature of pride. 'It is Pride,' he tells us, 'which has been the chief cause of misery in every nation and every family since the world began ... Pride always means enmity—it *is* enmity. And not only enmity between man and man,

---

4.   Svetlana Alliluyeva, *Only One Year*, trans. Paul Chavchavadze (New York: Harper & Row, 1969).

but enmity to God.'[5] Lewis also makes this observation: 'Pride gets no pleasure out of having something, only out of having more of it than the next man.'[6] This is the explanation for Stalin's lusts. He is proud, meaning he wants more than the next person. And being powerful enables him to achieve an extraordinary degree of such superiority, at least so he imagined.

Many captains of industry and corporate heads having achieved enormous wealth still want more. Why? In a word, power. Money can get you some things, but when you have more than you need then only one avenue is open to you: controlling other people. Such a quest for power is not limited to the grand schemes of politics and business. It occurs in families as well. How many husbands seek to dominate their families, however humble in material things? How many wives seek to manipulate their families, however modest their standing?

Can the downward spiral of power-mongering be broken? Is Christianity practical here? Certainly. An outstanding example of a good reversal of fortune, a breach with the lust for power, is the story of Alexandr Solzhenitsyn, the man who, more than perhaps any

---

5. C. S. Lewis, *Mere Christianity* (New York: Macmillan, 1943) p. 108.

6. Lewis, *Mere Christianity*, p. 107.

other single individual, was used to reveal the horrors of Soviet communism which led to its demise. Although a loyal Marxist and a former captain in the Red Army, Solzhenitsyn (1918–2008) had made critical comments about Stalin's leadership in World War II. He made these comments to a friend, sarcastically referring to Stalin as *Khozyain* (the 'proprietor'). He was sentenced to eight years in a labor camp. While in prison, he met a recent convert to Christianity from Judaism, Dr Boris Nikolayevich Kornfeld, who testified to him of his faith. One fateful night the doctor was beaten to death for no apparent reason. Deeply shaken, Solzhenitsyn began to ponder the meaning of this murder.

As he thought about conditions in the camp, he began to realize it was not only the prison guards who had let power go to their heads. It was each human being. It was himself. In his book *The Gulag Archipelago* he relates how when he was in the army he was no better than the henchmen in the gulag. He realized that the sin of power-mongering was an equal-opportunity disease. Here is how he puts it:

> It was granted to me to carry away from my prison years on my bent back, which nearly broke beneath its load, this essential experience: *how* a human being becomes evil and *how* good. In the intoxication of youthful successes I had felt myself to be infallible,

and I was therefore cruel. In the surfeit of power I was a murderer, and an oppressor. In my most evil moments I was convinced that I was doing good, and I was well supplied with systematic arguments. It was only when I lay there on rotting prison straw that I sensed within myself the first stirrings of good. Gradually it was disclosed to me that the line separating good and evil passes not through states, nor between classes, nor between political parties either—but right through every human heart—and through all human hearts. This line shifts. Inside us, it oscillates with the years. And even within hearts overwhelmed by evil, one small bridgehead of good is retained. And even in the best of all hearts, there remains ... an unuprooted small corner of evil.[7]

While we might want further elaboration on what he means by a nascent good within him, a generous reading simply sees a man beginning to understand his own cruelty, an understanding that led him back to the Orthodox Christian faith of his youth.

The Bible has a great deal to say about the proper and the improper exercise of power. Over and over it warns against thinking we can accomplish anything by our own capabilities (Deuteronomy 8:17; 9:4). The wrong use of power is an insidious gloom (Leviticus 26:19; Ezekiel 24:21; Luke 22:53; 1 John 5:19). But when we

7. Alexandr I. Solzhenitsyn, *The Gulag Archipelago 1918-1956: An Experiment in Literary Investigation III-IV*, trans. Thomas P. Whitney (New York: Harper & Row, 1975), p. 615.

acknowledge the true power of God and the authority of Jesus Christ over the earth, then our own exercise of authority can be managed, and not turn into a besetting sin (Exodus 9:16; Psalm 68:34; 145:11; Hebrews 1:3; Matthew 28:18-20). The gospel is indeed the power of God for salvation (Romans 1:16-17; 2 Peter 1:3). When it is preached that power is unleashed. Only when power comes upon us from on high, though, can we then work properly, not obsessively, for the coming of the Kingdom (Acts 1:8; 3:12; 4:33). Christianity is practical and can change power-mongers into God's power stewards.

8

Begetting Sins:
Addiction

BEING HOOKED

Somewhat different from our various temperamental sins is addictive behavior. All sins are related, but addictions are especially *besetting*. There are different kinds of addictions and they vary in their character. To list but a few: gambling, alcohol, over-eating, nicotine, pornography, over-work, substance abuse, and compulsive behavior. Today most medical resources will tell us that addiction is a disease. Parts of the disease model are useful. Like an illness, addictions often seem to control people and cures are hard to come by. There can be physical and even biological features for addictions. But most often these are symptoms, not causes. True enough there is a physical aspect to drug addiction, for example. Cocaine-dependency definitely has physical aspects: one is less and less able to resist or withdraw because, in part, our brains develop a need for the substance.

However, the most fundamental characteristic of addictions is spiritual. By that word I don't mean something mystical. I mean the explanation is in relation to God and the choices we make within that relationship. One of the most appropriate biblical themes which helps us understand addiction is idolatry.[1] As the Christian counselor Edward Welch puts it, idolatry 'captures both the in-control and out of control experiences of addictions.'[2] What he means is that on the one hand we have chosen to go outside of the appropriate boundaries of healthy life in the kingdom of God and take control and on the other hand, the addiction, whatever it may be, like the idol, takes control of us. Idolatry is a subject we do not study very often, but we ought to, since it is a besetting sin for people described throughout the Bible who are 'hooked' on the idol. While in the Old

1. In what follows I am deeply indebted to my colleague Edward T. Welch, academic dean and director of counseling at the Christian Counseling and Educational Foundation in Willow Grove, Pennsylvania. See his, *Addictions: A Banquet in the Grave: Finding Hope in the Power of the Gospel* (Phillipsburg: P & R Publishing, 2001).

2. Edward T. Welch, 'Addictions: New Ways of Seeing, New Ways of Walking Free', *Journal of Biblical Counseling*, 19/3 (Spring 2001), p. 20.

Testament idols were often visible, such as statues and the like, just because they are less palpable today does not mean they are not idols nonetheless. We can worship success, power over others, music, or other people (when it is the idolatry of another person psychologists often call it co-dependency).

Visible or not, idols come from the heart. As God explains to Ezekiel, telling him how the elders have gone astray, He says this: 'Son of man, these men have taken their idols into their hearts' (Ezekiel 14:3). The apostle Paul tells the Colossians to 'put to death therefore what is earthly in you: sexual immorality, impurity, passion, evil desire, and *covetousness, which is idolatry*' (Colossians 3:5). That is an important connection. Covetousness is at the root of all kinds of sins. Notice the sins he mentions here could all qualify as addictions, focusing as they do as much on desire as on activity. To use the language of Jonathan Edwards, the prominent American theologian of the eighteenth century, we may either set our *religious affections* on God, or on an earthly substitute.[3]

Characteristic of idols, therefore, is first their promise, then the momentary payoff, but finally their tyranny. Idols promise such pleasures as euphoria, security, sexual fulfillment, power, and the like. For

---

3. Jonathan Edwards, *The Religious Affections* (Mineola, NY: Dover Publications, reprint ed., 2013).

a while they seem to deliver. Some drugs do make you feel better, relieve you of pain, and give you a sense of freedom. Some wealth can give you a sense of security, and sense of power. Initially, adultery can be pleasurable. But then, soon, the idol takes you captive and won't want to let you out. You find you cannot live without the drug, or with less money, or without that illicit relationship. Very often your life falls apart, and you lose any control you ever had. Alcohol may literally kill you by destroying your liver. Addicted to money, you always want more but are less and less happy with what you have. Adulterers eventually will fail to live the double life and will be left with neither the legitimate spouse nor the illicit lover.[4]

Drug addiction

Are there answers for addicts? Certainly, just as there are answers for idolaters. Like the sins of the emotions, addictions need to be understood fully if there is to be any hope. Let's take the case of substance abuse. The problem is immense. I once was a school teacher in an affluent suburb of New York City. Although the young people I taught came from well-heeled families, there was a certain amount of emptiness. The vast amounts

---

4. Welch proposes the aptness of two other biblical images: the adulterer and the fool.

of wealth in the community could not compensate for the lack of meaning and fulfillment in the lives of the students; indeed they somehow were part of the problem. Several took to experimenting with cocaine and with heroine. I discovered there was a significant underworld of sellers who contacted the youth and sold them these drugs. I had the privilege of walking some of the students through to recovery, or finding a good rehab center for them.

What leads people, young or old, to practice substance abuse? There is not a single answer. People are most vulnerable to drug abuse between the ages of twelve and twenty, although there are some cases of adult experimentation leading to addiction. Here are some of the factors I found to be most prevalent: (1) moral and spiritual emptiness, (2) a dysfunctional family, (3) peer-pressure, (4) a cultural atmosphere which says, when you don't feel good, take a drug.[5] These factors do not *cause* drug abuse. Rather, the cause is human choice. Neither does the presence of these factors necessarily lead to drug abuse, nor does their absence guarantee its avoidance.

Patterns vary, but often the steps toward dependency involve experimentation, occasional use, regular use, or

---

5. The team Stephen Van Cleave, Walter Byrd, Kathy Revell find similar factors at work, in *Counseling for Substance Abuse and Addiction* (Waco, TX: Word Books, 1987); p. 19.

full-blown addiction.[6] What exactly is addiction? Drug dependence develops when the user desperately wants to get high or to avoid painful realities. Eventually the young person simply cannot live without the dope. And this is where things may lead to hope. Often, when someone truly reaches rock-bottom, or, the bottom falling out of the bottom, as one ministry puts it, then, rather like the prodigal son, he or she remembers there is a better way. When one is able to say, the drug is stronger than I, and I can no longer manage my life, then one is able to turn to God, and cry to Him 'out of the depths' (Psalm 130).

Many programs or methods seem plausible but in the end do not deliver what they promise. The administration at the school where I taught sponsored educational programs for the school. I remember one of them, which featured testimonies of former addicts, with graphic descriptions of their downhill journey toward despair and physical ailments of all kinds. The well-intentioned presenters thought they were conveying a message: this is what will happen to you if you mess with drugs; you will lose friends, career, your future. One of the students later became a good friend. A recovering drug addict, he explained to me

---

6.   Van Cleave, Byrd, and Revell, *Counseling for Substance Abuse and Addiction*, p. 29.

that during these programs he and several others were sitting in the front row and basically laughing inwardly. The testimonies struck them as naïve rather than cool, and they had the opposite of the intended effect. One of the students had joked that the only reason he might try to be clean is to be able to get up on the stage in front of a school and make dramatic speeches to impress everyone.

Where should one begin on the road to recovery? Only one place: admitting to God and then to others one's total helplessness, and indeed one's total guilt. Many addicts believe they can quit whenever they want. They delude themselves into thinking, tomorrow I will renounce drugs. But no amount of will power can achieve that, without the grace of God. Years ago there was a politically sanctioned program whose slogan was 'just say no!' Anyone who has struggled with dependency knows this can never work. When David had committed adultery and murder, he came to his senses when the prophet Nathan spoke to him about his treachery. Then he confessed to God: 'Have mercy on me, O God ... for I know my transgressions and my sin is ever before me. Against you, you only, have I sinned' (Psalm 51:1-4). David makes no attempt to cover up, nor to find excuses. He might have tried to explain to God that as the great king of Israel he had certain rights ... but the reality is, he was a miserable sinner. What follows is very pertinent to drug abuse. David asks for wisdom in the secret of his heart (v. 6). There is no medical model here. Nor a request for 'sex addiction therapy'. Instead, David asks for forgiveness and cleansing. One powerful portion of his prayer is, 'Let me hear joy and gladness; let the bones that you have broken rejoice' (v. 8). He is asking for his life to be rebuilt. Most often specific sinful acts result from patterns of living. Whatever these patterns may have been in David's life—complacency, pride, lust—he needed them treated. He even asks God to 'build up the walls of Jerusalem' (v. 18). Often, not only is the individual in need of reconstruction but also the people around him, people he has affected, or even led down the wrong path. Surely this is true of the drug-abuser. Victims include the family, the church, the school, and so forth. There are often legal consequences as well, since many have fed their addiction by illegal activities such as theft.

Is Christianity practical for breaking the bonds of drug-dependency? Certainly. Because at the heart of the Christian approach is the powerful grace of God. Such grace is offered in abundance in the gospel. Christ's death and resurrection avail for this besetting sin. Listen to how the New Testament characterizes that power. The gospel is the 'power of God for salvation'

(Romans 1:16). 'By the power of the Holy Spirit you may abound in hope' (Romans 15:13). The word of the cross is 'the power of God' (1 Corinthians 1:18). 'For the kingdom of God does not consist in talk but in power' (1 Corinthians 4:20). 'And God raised the Lord, and will also raise us up by his power' (1 Corinthians 6:14). 'For the weapons of our warfare are not of the flesh but have divine power to destroy strongholds' (2 Corinthians 10:4). 'That I may know him and the power of his resurrection' (Philippians 3:10). These are only a sampling of the many texts which proclaim the power of God to save us from any sin, besetting or otherwise.

The seventeenth-century Welsh theologian John Owen stressed the need to be and remain *violent* in the battle against addiction. Owen wrote a powerful treatise on *The Mortification of Sin*.[7] Only out-and-out battle can hope to keep sin under control. 'Sin will not only be striving, acting, rebelling, troubling, disquieting, but if let alone, if not continually mortified, it will bring forth great, cursed, scandalous, soul-destroying sins.'[8] We are easily deceived, he warns, by giving way to inveterateness (when sin long lies seemingly dormant in the heart), temporary relief, success, intellectual arguments, and

---

7.   John Owen, *The Mortification of Sin*, (1656, republished by Lexington, KY: Feathertrail Press, 2009).

8.   ibid., p. 15.

so forth. Owen strongly advocates the need for God's undeserved grace and the power of the Holy Spirit. Similarly Welch urges the addict (and, really, anyone else) to declare war against sin, to remain constantly vigilant, to 'show no mercy' to sinful desires, and the like.[9] And, like Owen, Welch preaches the all-sufficiency of grace in the fight against sin. No perfection in this life, and yet there will be progress.[10]

Victory for the recovering drug addict will depend not only on waging this spiritual battle, but on being placed in a context where support and accountability are constantly available. He or she needs to be surrounded by people who can give them tough love. The addict on the road to recovery will need a solid church, and special mentors to hold him or her accountable. Character formation, rather than mere techniques or disciplines, should be inculcated in these communities. In some cases treatment will require inpatient therapy or even residential programs. Van Cleave, Byrd and Revell recommend calling such programs 'habilitation' rather than 'rehabilitation' programs, on the basis that many drug users have never finished going through the normal growth process and need to learn to live for the

---

9. Welch, 'Addictions', pp. 25-7.

10. ibid., pp. 27-9.

first time.[11] There are a number of first-rate residential programs. Before sending someone there, however, it is important to investigate them thoroughly to make sure all the elements for a sound curriculum are present.

Is Christianity practical even in the very difficult case of drug addiction? Absolutely. It works because, while understanding the physical power of the dependence, it goes to the deeper spiritual root of the problem, much as we stressed in the case of Carl Jung's psychology earlier in chapter 2.

PORNOGRAPHY

One of the great blights in our so-called advanced societies is pornography. What is it? Simply put, pornography is the depiction of erotic behavior in pictures or writing meant to cause illicit sexual excitement. The qualifier 'illicit' helps guard against the idea that every description of erotic love is wrong. If that were the case we would have to excise the *Song of Songs* from our Bibles. And there exist novels, paintings and films that celebrate that love within marriage, which is the only proper place for it. Pornography, on the other hand, removes sexual love from that God-given setting and depicts it simply to incite lust in the reader or viewer. While pornography has been around since ancient civilizations, today it has

11. Stephen Van Cleave, Walter Byrd, Kathy Revell, op. cit., p. 137.

spread like wildfire through means such as the Internet. In the United States alone, 12 per cent of websites are pornographic. Revenue from internet pornography represents a staggering 2.84 billion dollars per year (4.9 worldwide).[12] Not only do Christians watch pornography but pastors and other leaders do as well. Not only do men, primarily, watch it, but now there is an increasing number of women who watch.

What is the power of this phenomenon? Sexuality is one of God's greatest gifts. Intended for our enjoyment within marriage, it is one of the highest forms of attraction between a man and a woman. And, of course, it is through physical union that children are born and the race perpetuated. From the early chapters of Genesis we see how beautiful is God's design. When Adam beheld Eve for the first time, he exclaimed: 'This is at last bone of my bones and flesh of my flesh ...' and the author adds: 'Therefore a man shall leave his father and his mother and hold fast to his wife, and they shall become one flesh' (Genesis 2:23-4). Thus, when God commanded mankind: 'Be fruitful and multiply and fill the earth and subdue it,' He gave marriage and family as the means to accomplish that mandate. It should not surprise us that sexual attraction has such a powerful appeal. Different

12. See [http://gizmodo.com/5552899/finally-some-actual-stats-on-internet-porn].

persons know different levels of sexual desire. For some it is most insistent. Paul recognizes the Corinthians' dilemma, answering their question about whether sexual relations were appropriate, even in a world where there is 'impending distress'. His answer is that for some, it is 'better to marry than to burn' (1 Corinthians 7:9, KJV). Accordingly neither spouse should 'deprive one another' except on rare occasions (1 Corinthians 7:5).

The best gifts become the most ugly in a fallen world. Worship becomes idolatry. Brotherly love becomes murder. Possessions turn to glittery excess. And sex becomes adultery. At the heart of marriage is covenant companionship (Proverbs 2:17). Adultery not only breaks the faithfulness but the companionship as well. While in pornography addiction there is no physical adultery, the parallels cannot be missed. When Jesus said: 'Everyone who looks at a woman with lustful intent has already committed adultery with her in his heart,' He is drawing the moral equivalency of intent and actuality. While to be sure pornography addiction is not exactly the same as real adultery with another spouse, it is drawing on the same intent.

Like other addictions there are a host of reasons why some people are drawn to pornography. Some have unmet needs for love and they try to satisfy it with images. Others, particularly young people, are fascinated by forbidden adventures. Still others simply have sexual desires that are insistent and they seek to satisfy them without the challenges of marriage. Also like other addictions there are all kinds of techniques and therapies which are ineffective or of limited value. Self-discipline, filters, accountability relationships, and so forth may be of some help but they do not go to the root of the problem. Sometimes men believe certain lies and cannot get free because of their deception. For example, they lull themselves into complacency by the false *dictum*, this happens to other people, not to me. Or, worse, we may start to think, I can't help it; it's not so bad, really.[13] For pornography is indeed persistent, but to leave a door open such as this goes against what Owen and Welch have taught us about vigilance.

The root of the problem is a relationship with God gone awry. And because of that we try to satisfy our relational needs illicitly. What we said about idolatry earlier certainly applies here. Pornography promises instant gratification, it delivers pleasure in the short term, and then you are hooked, and find yourself less and less satisfied. If unchecked the pornography habit not only affects the individual but others around him. The addict practices

---

13. There are numerous resources for the pornography problem. One might consult an illuminating article about the problem of deception by J. Alasdair Groves, 'Exposing the Lies of Pornography and Counseling the Men Who Believe Them', *Journal of Biblical Counseling* 27/1 (2013), pp. 7-25.

more and more deception, and begins to lead a double life. Just as the idolater thinks he is just being a little inconsistent at first, or keeps what the French call *mon péché mignon* ('my cute sin') in his comportment, so the pornography addict tells himself, there's no real harm if I just click on this site once, just to see. And just as the idolater finds himself more and more dependent on the idol, so the pornography addict eventually cannot break with it.[14] His family, his friends, his colleagues at work will be affected.

With the primary relationship with God not right, every other relationship suffers, including the actors, if that is what they are, on the screen. Clicking on a site to look at a woman, or at some clip, contributes to the dehumanization of the persons involved. They may have chosen to be there, but they are paid for, often coerced by the pimps and gangsters who sponsor them. Pornography is largely a shady, if not criminal industry. Despite attempts by 'soft' porn companies such as *Playboy* to make exposing young women to customers appear wholesome and natural, there is nothing wholesome about it. Often a young woman's life can be ruined by going down the dark path of such prostitution.

---

14. Some of the most helpful resources on idolatry come from Timothy Keller, *Counterfeit Gods: The Empty Promises of Money, Sex and Power, and the Only Hope that Matters* (New York: Penguin/Dutton, 2009).

So, is Christianity practical in liberating people from the pornography addiction? Very much so. First, because it recognizes the deep root of the problem to be spiritual, not biological. To access pornographic sites is to say to God, in effect, you did not provide for me in this area of sexual need. To be sure, God's provision is not always going to be through a blissful marriage. Indeed married people can become pornography addicts as much as anyone. God may call you to be celibate and continent. But it is only when you turn to God 'out of the depths' and cry out to Him for mercy, and for a contented relationship with Him that other relationships including the sexual one will find its proper place.

Second, because the Bible is utterly realistic about both the problem and its resolution. Page after page in the Bible we find acknowledgment of human weakness, including in the area of sexuality. The greatest king in the Old Testament committed adultery and murder. The opening of the book of Proverbs likens folly to a seductive woman. Israel's unfaithfulness is compared to a harlot. And yet, at the same time, forgiveness and restoration are real and close at hand. David was forgiven and restored. The young sage in Israel is instructed on how to avoid the seductress. Israel was restored. We sometimes imagine God must be tired of us. We've sinned one time too many. That is because we ignore the depths of His love and the power of the gospel to save and to forgive, over and over again.

Pornography addicts ought to seek help, and yet because this is one of the most shameful and embarrassing sins, they are reluctant to go for counseling. But the best counselors are approachable and compassionate. They will not blow your cover. I am a Presbyterian minister, and so I must attend presbytery meetings regularly. A while ago we had a teaching session on the problem of pornography. The young man who led it was himself a recovering user. He reminded us that there could be no better place to go for help than to fellow ministers. He advised finding at least one colleague with whom to stay accountable. Far better to confide in a friend than to get caught and create a scandal.

When the regular church facilities are not enough then a number of ministries specializing in sexual brokenness are available for help. One of them, Harvest, based in Philadelphia, has a most encouraging record of victory stories not just over pornography addictions but other kinds of sexual sins, including adultery, homosexuality, self-indulgence, etc. The staff workers at Harvest will be quick to tell you there is failure as well. Yet they have seen the effects of honest confrontation, and gospel-driven remedies. Christ died for all varieties of sins. His death is effectual over sexual sins as well.

VICTORY OVER ADDICTIONS

These are but two examples of addictive sins. Many more can be cited: gambling, nicotine, food, etc. Although the different types have somewhat different characteristics, yet the diagnosis and the cure are the same. Addictions are slaveries to idols. They may be many other things, but those are at the core. A word of warning: perhaps more than any other kind of sin, addictions involve deception. Because of that, it is easy to think once initial victory has been achieved that it's all over. No more drugs, no more porn, no more nicotine. Such a victory is remarkable indeed. And yet, as many addicts know, it is all too easy to fall back into destructive patterns. When we do, not only can we become hooked again, but we may be very, very discouraged. At this point two things should be remembered. First, the gospel of Jesus Christ is still truly the power of God to break with idols (Romans 1:16; 1 Corinthians 1:18, 24; 2:5; 6:14; 15:24; 2 Corinthians 10:4; Ephesians 1:19). Victory can occur once, twice, three times, and many, many more. The very nature of addiction is that it 'crouches at the door' (Genesis 4:7). Very likely (though not necessarily) subsequent falls will occur. But the Lord, whose loving inclination is always to forgive, will also grant His power to progress substantially over the patterns.

Second, and this is crucial, unless we replace the

idol with something positive, it will come back to visit us. Jesus tells of a demon leaving a person, but then returning with seven others to possess him. He compares it to finding a house swept and put in order, all the more ready to receive the evil spirits (Matthew 12:43-5). Overcoming an addiction should be more than emptying one's house of the idol. The house must be filled again. With what? With the presence of the living God, who alone can satisfy all our longings. Jesus promised that after He had gone, He would send the Holy Spirit to live in us (John 14:17; 2 Corinthians 1:22; James 4:5). When He comes to live in us, He brings us up into God's own dwelling place, where we may 'gaze upon the beauty of the LORD' forever (Psalm 27:4). You see, the addiction is but a poor, enslaving counterfeit for that which truly satisfies. Here is how C. S. Lewis puts it: 'It would seem that Our Lord finds our desires not too strong, but too weak. We are half-hearted creatures, fooling about with drink and sex and ambition when infinite joy is offered us, like an ignorant child who wants to go on making mud pies in a slum because he cannot imagine what is meant by the offer of a holiday at the sea. We are far too easily pleased.'[15]

---

15. C. S. Lewis, *The Weight of Glory and Other Addresses* (Grand Rapids: Eerdmans, 1965), pp. 1-2.

9

Is it Beyond Me?

RELIEF FROM SUFFERING

Every true Christian will suffer. That's a promise (Acts 14:22; 1 Peter 1:6; 4:12). Every form of suffering tells the same story: we have gone astray from God, our great shepherd, and as a consequence we wander in misery and affliction. The consequence is both 'natural', since refusing to love God is a miserable affair, and 'supernatural', since God is also judge, and turns His face against rebels. Yet there are types of suffering that are relatively light, easier to bear, and others that are rather more relentless.

For convenience let us isolate two kinds of serious afflictions. The first is physical disease. We might think of such diseases as Alzheimer's, or cancer. Anyone who has witnessed a loved one degenerate through Alzheimer's or dementia will agree with Czeslaw Milosz: 'Wise thoughts fail in its presence,' and 'starry skies go out.' When chronicling the slow, downhill journey of his wife's Alzheimer's, John Bayley, the eminent British literary critic, compared her face to a mask. Iris Murdoch (1919–1999), herself a considerable novelist and philosopher, was diagnosed with the disease six years before her death.[1] Bayley related how she did not know anymore that she had written twenty-six remarkable novels and books on philosophy. Everything takes time. Though somehow her unique personality was not lost, yet her days were a sort of despair. She could smile, but only perfunctorily. Bayley compared Iris's face to a lion face, with 'a leonine impassivity which does remind one of the king of beasts, and the way his broad expressionless mask is represented in painting or sculpture.' Still, the image of God in Iris refused to be extinguished. Bayley remarked on how she would have flashes of coherence, of love and of humor.

Cancer can similarly beset its victim for a long time before the end, yet without necessarily the loss of the mind. My friend David Calhoun has survived throat cancer several times. In his reflections he combines sober realism with the hope of the gospel. One source

1. See John Bayley, *Elegy for Iris* (New York: Picador/St Martin's Press, 1999).

of solace for him is poetry. He describes going through the valley of the shadow of death (Psalm 23). It is 'a place of darkness, sadness, affliction and trial,' he says.[2] Yet we must traverse it if we are to get to the other side, to the banquet and the horn of plenty. Calhoun loves the metaphysical poet George Herbert. His poem 'Bitter-Sweet' well captures the ambiguity of sorrow and joy in the Lord during the experience of suffering:

> Ah my dear angry Lord,
> Since thou dost love, yet strike;
> Cast down, yet help afford; Sure I will do the like.
>
> I will complain, yet praise;
> I will bewail, approve;
> And all my sour-sweet days
> I will lament and love.

Calhoun has learned to ask for comfort rather than deliverance from the troubles of life. During one experience of chemotherapy, one that nearly killed him, he remembered a semi-humorous poem by Robert Herrick:

> When the artless doctor sees
> No one hope, but of his fees,

2.   David B. Calhoun, 'Poems in the Park: My Cancer and God's Grace' in *Suffering and the Goodness of God*, Christopher W. Morgan & Robert A. Peterson, eds, vol. 1 (Wheaton: Crossway Books, 2008), p. 195.

And his skill runs on the lees,
Sweet Spirit, comfort me![3]

Calhoun hastens to point out that most of his attendants were both skilled and humane. But on this one occasion when they were not, it seemed that a little humor was somehow appropriate. Still, throughout his ordeal, he thought more and more about the God who Himself became a man of suffering. In the words of William Blake:

Think not thou canst sigh a sigh
And thy maker is not by;
Think not thou canst weep a tear
And thy maker is not near.[4]

These personal examples of disease are but one aspect of the universal plight of mankind.

A second kind of example is not related to disease as such, but to human cruelty. This is often person to person. An abusive husband; a bully at school; slandering a colleague. Deception, manipulation, power-plays, these are the common experiences of the bulk of humanity.

This plight can also be on a much larger scale. Suffering on a massive scale is the stuff of our times. We can think of the genocide by the Hutus of the Tutsi

---

3. Calhoun, 'Poems in the Park: My Cancer and God's Grace' in *Suffering and the Goodness of God*, p. 198.

4. ibid., p. 201.

people in Rwanda in 1994. Or of the mass killings of the Cambodians by the Khmer Rouge, led by Pol Pot between 1975 and 1979. Or, again, of the ethnic cleansing campaign in Bosnia by the Army of the Republika Srpska.

WHERE DO WE FIND ANSWERS?

The list goes on. Where do we turn? Perhaps surprisingly, the first thing to say here is that the Bible authorizes not just anger but outrage at the presence of such evil and suffering. When Jacqueline Kennedy looked over at her blood-stained husband, seconds after his assailant shot him in the head, her only two words were, 'No, no!' Denial? Anger? Outrage? All of the above. She is in good company. Throughout the Bible the most godly people complain to the Lord, and are not condemned for it. The Psalmists regularly ask: 'How long, O LORD? Will you forget me forever? How long will you hide your face from me?' (Psalm 13:1; 74:10; 79:5; 80:4). At times the complaint is painfully honest: 'How long must your servant endure? When will you judge those who persecute me?' (Psalm 119:84) 'You who are of purer eyes than to see evil and cannot look at wrong, why do you idly look at traitors and are silent when the wicked swallows up the man more righteous than he?' (Habakkuk 1:13).

These human reactions are authorized because God Himself reacts the same way to human suffering and injustice. God is angry at the false shepherds who lead the people astray as well as the people whose hearts are so hardened they cannot do any good (Zechariah 7:12; 10:3). God is especially angry at crimes that are covered up. Isaiah's prophecy against Ariel, the symbolic name for Jerusalem, includes fierce condemnation against those who try to conduct their crimes in secret: 'Woe to those who go to great depths to hide their plans from the LORD, who do their works in darkness and think, "Who sees us? Who will know?" (Isaiah 29:15).

We often think of Jesus as meek and mild. Those adjectives have more to do with Hallmark cards than with the New Testament. Once He cleansed a leper of his disease in the synagogue and on the Sabbath (Mark 3:1-4). The fuming religious leaders resented this apparent breach of the religious law. Jesus asked them whether it was right to do good or to do harm on the Sabbath. 'And he looked around at them with anger, grieved at their hardness of heart' (v. 5). When Jesus saw Mary and many other Jews weeping at the tomb of Lazarus, dead for four days, He 'was deeply moved in his spirit and greatly troubled' (John 11:33). The Greek word translated 'deeply moved' means 'to snort with anger', as would a wild beast when provoked. And the word for 'greatly troubled' means an inward commotion, a deep distress. Jesus was furious at the death of His friend. He was livid before human suffering.

It is no good denying human suffering or death. Though it stares us in the face we would rather not look at it. Every village has its cemeteries, every hospital its morgue. Death is universal (Romans 5:14-18; 1 Corinthians 15:22). The strongest can prolong life, but no one can avoid death. We bring our years to an end like a sigh (Psalm 90:9). All the toil of our hand, the author of Ecclesiastes tells us, is but 'vanity and a striving after wind' when done only from a this-worldly perspective (Ecclesiastes 2:11).

How is this hopeful? Because only when we know the worst can we begin to look for answers. If we are merely confused, we can look for order. If we are merely ignorant, we can find knowledge. But if we are dead ... we need something far more radical. We need resurrection.

And this is precisely what the Bible gives us. Lazarus was dead. Not asleep, nor in a swoon. He was without life for four days. But Jesus Christ, with the same voice He used to bring the world into being, the same word that holds everything together, cried out with a loud voice, 'Lazarus, come out' (John 11:43). And he did. He who was dead came back to life. How could this be? Because in a few days after this event Jesus would Himself die a horrible death, and lie buried in His own tomb for two days. And on the third day, He would rise again, because the purpose of Jesus' death was to take upon Himself the ultimate cause of death: our sin. He died in order to be punished for our guilt. 'For our sake he made him to be sin who knew no sin, so that in him we might become the righteousness of God' (2 Corinthians 5:21).

CONCLUSION

While the gospel does not give us all the answers to why this disease and why that affliction may visit, it does tell us that all suffering has been overcome, through the suffering of God's only Son. And while it does not tell us in great detail what life everlasting will look like, it does tell us it will have incomparable beauty, such that 'the sufferings of this present time are not worth comparing with the glory that is to be revealed to us' (Romans 8:18).

We come back to the beginning. Certainly, 'Christianity is not true because it works; it works because it is true.' The main reason to believe in the Christian faith is not that it is practical. We don't commend the Christian faith because somehow it pays off. Many religions have at least short-term payoffs. And yet there must be a sense in which the gospel produces results. Call them the necessary consequences of the Christian religion. If it made no difference, either in the world or in individual hearts, then it would have little more appeal than a pure mathematical formula: entirely valid, even elegant, no doubt, but without observable consequences in the real world.

More important, it would not live up to its own claims, since, as we have already underscored, Jesus promised to build His church. He further and quite often compared receiving the gospel authentically to bearing fruit. A tree that does not bear fruit is cut down and thrown away (Matthew 7:19). But a true disciple will bear fruit 'thirtyfold and sixtyfold and a hundredfold' (Mark 4:20). A modern way of putting this, though far more banal, is to look for *measurable results*.

An interesting incident occurred in ancient Thessalonica. Paul and Silas had come there to preach the crucified, risen Christ. While a good many people received the message and followed them, a number of opponents tried to discredit them by calling them treasonable. They said, meaning it negatively, that these men had 'turned the world upside down' (Acts 17:6). But there is a sense in which the Christian message ought to turn the world upside down, challenging its injustices, meeting its many illnesses with healing power, and changing lives for the good. In these pages we have looked briefly at a few of the places where this has occurred. We looked at world-changing Christian artisans of peace working in what looked like intractable circumstances. We looked at pioneers of health care initiatives by biblically-based agents. We also examined the more personal spiritual issues of unanswered prayer, persistent sins and addictions, and saw that there are answers even for some of the most stubborn evils, just as there are for sufferings of all kinds.

What we have tried to argue is that while all kinds of questions remain, the gospel is 'the power of God for salvation to everyone who believes' (Romans 1:16). Salvation here is meant to be understood in a far broader sense than a passage to heaven, though it surely is that. Indeed, salvation is more extensive than rescue, even rescue from sin, which, of course, it is. Salvation is deliverance from the guilt and pollution of sin in which the human race finds itself. Salvation overcomes death itself. But it is also a reorientation of life, all of life, into the ways of liberty. Deepest of all, salvation restores us to fellowship with God Himself. It puts us into an eternal communion and conversation with the Lord, one which has implications for every aspect of our lives. Salvation brings truth into our lives, but also power, the power to change everything that is distorted and make it straight.

You may be looking at the world and wondering, where can this truth and power be found? There is plenty to be alarmed about. But when you look carefully, you will see much to be encouraged about as well. We have written about some of them. And there are many more. At the same time, there is much work left to be done. The sober realism of the Christian message prevents us from the error of sentimentality. But the resurrection power of the gospel prevents us from the opposite error of cynicism or despair. Here is how Paul experienced it:

> But we have this treasure in jars of clay, to show that the surpassing power belongs to God and not to us. We are afflicted in every way, but not crushed; perplexed, but not driven to despair; persecuted, but not forsaken; struck down, but not destroyed; always carrying in the body the death of Jesus, so that the life of Jesus may also be manifested in our bodies. For we who live are always being given over to death for Jesus' sake, so that the life of Jesus also may be manifested in our mortal flesh. So death is at work in us, but life in you. (2 Corinthians 4:7-12)

Not all of us are called in this life to the depths of suffering or the heights of glory as the apostle Paul was. But all of us are called both to suffer and to know the goodness of God at our own levels (Psalm 34:8).

Is Christianity practical? G. K. Chesterton put it this way: 'Christianity has not been tried and found wanting, it has been found difficult and not tried.' The great challenge for our generation, then, is to try the Christian faith and see that, though difficult, it will not be found wanting.

Further Reading

Jonathan Aitken, *John Newton: From Disgrace to Amazing Grace* (Wheaton: Crossway, 2013).

Eberhard Bethge, *Dietrich Bonhoeffer: Theologian, Christian, Man for His Times: A Biography*, rev. ed., (Minneapolis, Fortress Press, 2000).

Michael Cassidy, *A Witness Forever* (London: Hodder & Stoughton, 1995).

Joni Eareckson, *Joni: An Unforgettable Story* (Grand Rapids: Zondervan, 1976).

Gillian Gill, *Nightingales: The Extraordinary Upbringing and Curious Life of Florence Nightingale* (New York: Random House, 2005).

James Turner Johnson, *Morality and Contemporary Warfare* (New Haven: Yale University Press, 1999).

Douglas Johnston & Cynthia Sampson, eds, *Religion, the Missing Dimension of Statecraft* (New York: Oxford University Press, 1995).

Ken Sande, *The Peacemaker: A Biblical Guide to Resolving Personal Conflict*, 3rd ed. (Grand Rapids: Baker Books, 2004).

Corrie Ten Boom, *The Hiding Place* (Grand Rapids: Baker/Chosen Books, 1971).

Richard Winter, *The Roots of Sorrow: Reflections on Depression and Hope* (Basingstoke: Marshall Pickering, 1986).

The Big Ten
Critical Questions Answered

This is a Christian apologetics series which aims to address ten commonly asked questions about God, the Bible, and Christianity. Each book, while easy to read, is challenging and thought-provoking, addressing subjects ranging from hell to science. A good read whatever your present opinions.

The books in this series are:

Christian Focus Publications

Our mission statement –

STAYING FAITHFUL

In dependence upon God we seek to impact the world through literature faithful to His infallible Word, the Bible. Our aim is to ensure that the Lord Jesus Christ is presented as the only hope to obtain forgiveness of sin, live a useful life and look forward to heaven with Him.

Our books are published in four imprints:

CHRISTIAN
FOCUS

Popular works including biographies, commentaries, basic doctrine and Christian living.

CHRISTIAN
HERITAGE

Books representing some of the best material from the rich heritage of the church.

MENTOR

Books written at a level suitable for Bible College and seminary students, pastors, and other serious readers. The imprint includes commentaries, doctrinal studies, examination of current issues and church history.

CF4•K

Children's books for quality Bible teaching and for all age groups: Sunday school curriculum, puzzle and activity books; personal and family devotional titles, biographies and inspirational stories – because you are never too young to know Jesus!

Christian Focus Publications Ltd,
Geanies House, Fearn, Ross-shire,
IV20 1TW, Scotland, United Kingdom.
www.christianfocus.com